The Hope of Christ's Second Coming

The Hope of Christ's Second Coming

How Is It Taught in Scripture? and Why?

Samuel P. Tregelles, LL.D.

Strong Tower Publishing
Bellefonte, PA

Copyright© 2006 Strong Tower Publishing

All rights reserved. No part of this book may be reproduced without permission from the publisher, except for brief portions, which may be used for literary review. No portions of this book may be reproduced, copied, or stored by electronic or mechanical means without permission from the publisher.

Strong Tower Publishing
P.O. Box 973
Milesburg, PA 16853
www.strongtowerpublishing.com

ISBN 0-9772883-0-7
LCCN 2006924175

All scripture quotations taken from the King James Version

Contents

Publisher's Foreword — 7

Preface to the Second Edition — 9
CECIL YATES BISS, 1886

Chapter 1:	Obedience to Revealed Truth	11
Chapter 2:	The Question Stated, Matthew 24	13
Chapter 3:	The Visible Coming in Clouds, Acts 1	17
Chapter 4:	Knowledge of Prophetic Details Not Necessary	21
Chapter 5:	An Interval Taught by the Lord	25
Chapter 6:	Apostolic Testimony	29
Chapter 7:	The Book of Revelation and the First Resurrection	35
Chapter 8:	The 'Secret Rapture' Explained	41
Chapter 9:	The 'Secret Rapture': Its Origin	43
Chapter 10:	The Jewish 'Waste-paper Basket'	47
Chapter 11:	Analogy Is Not Necessarily Proof	51
Chapter 12:	1 Corinthians 15:51–54 and Isaiah 25:7–8 Compared	55
Chapter 13:	Tribulation Arguments Reconsidered	57
Chapter 14:	The Double: 'Two Jewish Remnants'	63

Chapter 15:	Corroborative Passages: 'Wheat and Tares'	67
Chapter 16:	'Parousia' and 'Epiphaneia'	69
Chapter 17:	Watch!	75
Chapter 18:	Are Signs Jewish?	79
Chapter 19:	Secret Rapture — Scriptures Contradictory	81
Chapter 20:	The Day of the Lord: Canticles and Apocalypse	87
Chapter 21:	'Times and Seasons'	95
Chapter 22	Sentiment and Emotion: The Truth of God	99
Chapter 23	'The Resurrection of the Just'	111
Chapter 24	The Hope	117

Appendixes

Appendix A	The Jewish 'Waste-paper Basket'	129
Appendix B	Analogies	131
Appendix C	Jewish Aspects of the Tribulation in Palestine	133
Appendix D	Five Aspects of the Kingdom of God	135
Appendix E	Responsibility for False Teaching	137
Appendix F	'A Thief in the Night'	139
Appendix G	Remarks on and Summary of the Apocalypse	141
Appendix H	Job Loved 'The Appearing'	145
Appendix J	The 'Theory' Leads Away From Close Bible Study	147

Preface to the Second Edition

For some years past, this valuable book—the first edition of which was issued in the year 1864—has been out of print; and it now appears to be a duty, in response to the request of many who greatly value it, to issue a second edition. This is the more needful as the errors of prophetic teaching which it was written to meet, have suffered no decadence, but, on the contrary, have developed ampler proportions, and extended over a wider sphere of influence than could have been supposed possible at first by those who, like Dr. Tregelles, were acquainted with the circumstances of their origin and early dissemination.

It is not, however, surprising when we remember that every day is bringing us nearer to the "end of the age"—the period when right prophetic instruction will be most needed by the people of God, and when also the delusive power of the great Adversary shall be most put forth. "Now the Spirit speaketh expressly that in the latter times some shall depart from the faith" (1 Tim. 4:1). "For that day shall not come except there come THE APOSTASY (ἡ ἀποστασια) first, and that Man of Sin be revealed, the Son of Perdition...whose coming is after the working of Satan, with all power and signs, and lying wonders, and with all deceivableness of unrighteousness in them that perish (2 Thess. 2 3:9,10).

The Hope of Christ's Second Coming

    The duty of preparing these pages for the press has been committed to me; and it is with feelings of the deepest gratitude to God, and, under Him, to the human instrument, that I have undertaken it. For this pamphlet was the means first used, now eighteen years ago, to deliver my mind from the influence of much false prophetic teaching, and to guide me to the Scriptures for instruction upon these subjects.

    This Edition is a reprint of the former one. An Appendix has been added, containing a few notes on points upon which it seemed desirable to enlarge because of more recent developments of the original errors. For these notes the Editor alone is responsible.

—Cecil Yates Biss
London, W.
October, 1886

S. P. Tregelles

Publisher's Foreword

The origins and teachings of the pretribulation rapture view are under much debate. Pretribulationists hold that theirs is the view of the early church, that this interpretation goes back to the apostolic fathers. Critics of pretribulationism, on the other hand, feel that the view's origins are relatively recent, originating in Great Britain in the early 1800s, either with the Irvingites or the Darbyites from 1827–1830.

It's a feisty debate, so when I was handed a copy of *The Hope of Christ's Second Coming*, written by S. P. Tregelles in 1964, I was riveted. Here was a well-respected theologian reacting to the pretribulation rapture view, not 200 years after it first gained popularity, but in the very moments it was taking hold. A biblical scholar and theologian who lived from 1813–1875, S. P. Tregelles was well acquainted with the centuries of Christian scholarship and recognized the "secret rapture" as a new interpretation of scripture, about which he was sufficiently alarmed to write this response in 1864.

Samuel Prideaux Tregelles was born in Wodehouse Place near Falmouth in 1813 and died in Plymouth on April 24th 1875. He was known both as a biblical scholar and a hymnist. His chief critical works include *Hebrew Reading Lessons*; *Prophetic Visions in the Book of Daniel*;

THE HOPE OF CHRIST'S SECOND COMING

Hebrew and Chaldee Lexicon; The Original Language of St. Matthew's Gospel; The Jansenists; Hebrew Psalter; Defence of the Book of Daniel; Hebrew Grammar; Collation of the Text of Griesbach and Others; Fragments of St. Luke (Codex Zacynthius); and *The Hope of Christ's Second Coming.*

    S. P. Tregelles was also a respected textual critic of the ancient biblical manuscripts. Among his recognized works are *An Account of the Printed Text of the Greek New Testament, with Remarks on Its Revision Upon Critical Principles,* published in 1854; *An Introduction to the Textual Criticism of the New Testament,* published in 1856; and *The Greek New Testament, Edited From Ancient Authorities,* published in 1857.

    Particularly relevant to the rapture debate is that Tregelles did not view the rise of the "secret rapture" teaching from afar. Having been born and raised in London, he watched the rise of this view in his own backyard. Thus, his view on its origins, theology, and rise to popularity provide a particularly poignant and relevant addition to the debate that rages to this day.

    In most cases, this current edition maintains the original punctuation and grammar as used by S. P. Tregelles in order to preserve the distinctive nineteenth century tone and style. However, minor edits have been made as necessary to maintain accuracy and consistency in punctuation and formatting.

    H. L. Nigro
    March, 2006

S. P. Tregelles

Chapter 1
Obedience to Revealed Truth

Behold He cometh with clouds, and every eye shall see Him . . . Even so, Amen. (Rev. 1:7)

The only means that we have of learning anything respecting the coming of our Lord, is from the teaching of Holy Scripture inspired by the Holy Ghost. Had the Scripture been silent we should have known nothing on the subject; on any points as to which Scripture is silent we do know nothing; but where the Scripture has spoken, we have as learners to receive what it teaches us; and if we shut our ears to this revelation, we are setters aside of the truth of God; or if we substitute our own speculations (however unconsciously) we are adding to what God has revealed.

If there are points which the Scripture does not clearly reveal, there may be differences of opinion; but where the Word of God definitely speaks, there we have simply to listen and to learn. We have not to inquire the use of what has been revealed before we consent to be learners; but taking the place of those willing to be taught, we have afterwards to seek Divine instruction as to the use of whatever the Spirit of God thus sets before us. We have first to know revealed truth as given by God for purposes

The Hope of Christ's Second Coming

that must be wise, and afterwards we may grow in the apprehension of its practical and moral bearing.

Before the first advent of Christ there had been the revelation concerning Him in promise and prophecy, and this, too, in very minute details: the family from which He should spring was foretold; His birth-place; the period in which He should come (as measured from a decree to restore and to build Jerusalem); His miracles, His teaching, His rejection, His crucifixion, death, and burial; His vicarious sacrifice; His resurrection; His ascension to the right hand of God the Father, and His tarriance seated there until His enemies shall be made His footstool. All these leading incidents connected with His coming (as well as many that are more minute) were given in ancient prophecy; but so little were they heeded, that the claims of Jesus of Nazareth to be the Messiah were denied because they were really in accordance with what the Scripture had foretold. "We know this man whence He is; but when Christ cometh no man knoweth whence He is" (John 7:27). This may be a warning to us as to the use which we make of those prophecies which deal with our hopes. The severe truth of God's revealed Word will clash harshly (if judged according to natural feelings) with everything that is tinctured with religious sentimentalism or with speculation, however refined, and however seemingly spiritual.

To those who hold as conclusive the words of the Lord Jesus, and the teaching of the Holy Ghost through apostles and prophets, I wish to address the inquiry, How is the second coming of Christ set forth in Holy Scripture? and why?

S. P. Tregelles

Chapter 2
The Question Stated, Matthew 24

There were with the Lord Jesus on the Mount of Olives, a few days before He suffered, a portion of that Church which He desired to instruct: whatever He then said to Peter, Andrew, James, and John, was not addressed to them for themselves merely, but to them as a portion of that one body to which, amongst other endowments, there had been given corporate hopes; that is, expectations not confined to individuals merely, not mere promises to be fulfilled to persons then living, but a hope belonging to a body as such, the visible accomplishment of which should take place in the days of certain of that body living in some one age. And thus the Lord Jesus in that prophetic discourse applies the terms "ye" and "you," not to the four disciples who had questioned Him as individuals, but to the Church of the first-born as one body, and having one hope, of which those four were representatives. Thus when He says, "When ye therefore shall see the abomination of desolation" (Matt. 24:15), "If they shall say unto you, Behold, He is in the desert, go not forth; behold, He is in the secret chambers, believe it not; for as the lightning," etc. (verses 26, 27). He specially, of course, regards those to whom His words would be applicable from the age in which they should live, and from their location and circumstances. But lest any should say that these things related to persons then living, merely as individuals, or lest in any other way they should avoid the force of the corporate "ye," our Lord in the same discourse adds, "What I say unto you, I say unto all, Watch" (Mark 13:37).

Now the questions put to the Lord Jesus by the disciples, and His reply to them, had to do with His coming in glory. They say, "What shall be the sign of Thy coming, and of the end of the world [age]?"[1] (Matt. 24:3). If, then, we would be rightly instructed as to these things, we are called on to take heed to His reply. In His answer, He first tells His disciples of many and various intervening events; deceivers should arise; there should be commotions amongst the nations—persecutions of the faithful servants of Christ—and the preaching of the Gospel should be carried out as a witness amongst all nations: all this must precede the end, and, in fact, must continue up to the end. The words, "the end is not yet" (verse 6)... "and then shall the end come" (verse 14), are of especial importance and weight as to this.

Whatever be the moral bearing of the hope of the coming of our Lord, He regarded it as being in nowise impaired by the knowledge which He himself gave of events that would intervene; for He taught such preceding events in answer to the inquiry of the disciples. If, then, we were to say that a belief in intervening events interferes

---

[1] "It is certainly a question whether we might not have made more use of 'age' in our version (for *αἰών*)...'age' may sound to us inadequate now; but it is quite possible that, so used, it would little by little have expanded, and acquired a larger, deeper meaning than it now possesses." (Abp. Trench; *Synonyms of the New Testament*. Part the Second. 1863, p. 32.)

with the hope of the coming of the Lord, or contradicts it, we must have adopted some incorrect opinion respecting it. The point now to be noticed is, not whether certain predicted events have now been accomplished, but whether the knowledge of such intervening events dims the hope of the second appearing of Christ. I shall have occasion subsequently to notice some of the particulars of this prophetic discourse: it is evident, on simply reading the inspired record of what our Lord then taught, that it sets before the believing people of Christ the hope that He shall Himself come "in the clouds of heaven with power and great glory;" that then "He shall send forth His angels with a great sound of a trumpet, and they shall gather together His elect from the four winds, from the one end of heaven to the other;" that before this coming there "shall be great tribulation, such as was not from the beginning of the world to this time, no, nor ever shall be;" and that the parable of the fig-tree is given us that we may learn how to watch and to wait. We have, in fact, to expect the Lord as He has promised to come, and in no other way.

The Hope of Christ's Second Coming

S. P. Tregelles

Chapter 3
The Visible Coming in Clouds, Acts 1

The apostles, forty days after the Lord's resurrection, accompanied Him to the Mount of Olives, and when they had received from Him His charge that they were to be witnesses for Him "unto the uttermost part of the earth," His ascension took place; "while they beheld He was taken up, and a cloud received Him out of their sight" (Acts 1:9). But while they were thus left, He was mindful of them; the two in white apparel, who appeared to them, directed them onward to the day of His coming again: "This same Jesus, which is taken up from you into heaven, shall so come in like manner as ye have seen Him go into heaven." These words, with the previous mention of the cloud by which the apostles had seen Him received out of their sight, appear to be intended to lead them, and to lead us, to consider the definite promises and prophecies which had been given of His coming in the clouds of heaven. They might remember Dan. 7:13: "I saw in the night visions, and, behold, one like the Son of Man came with the clouds of heaven, and came to the Ancient of days, and they brought Him near before Him; and there was given Him dominion, and glory, and a kingdom," etc. This scene is not actually the second advent of Christ, but that which is seen in heaven as immediately preceding it; when a certain power of blasphemy upon earth, which up to that time has persecuted the saints of the Most High, is judged, and when Christ is coming forth to take the kingdom. It is to this scene in Daniel that our Lord refers, in the various places in which He speaks of His own future coming "with the clouds of heaven": these clouds were the accompaniment of His appearing in glory so soon as He has received the investiture of this kingdom.

Our Lord, in His discourse on the Mount of Olives, in speaking of what should be "immediately after the tribulation of those days," specifies the darkening of the sun and moon, etc.: "And then shall appear the sign of the Son of man in heaven, and then shall all the tribes of the earth mourn, and they shall see the Son of man coming in the clouds of heaven with power and great glory" (Matt. 24:30). This, then, was the expectation of the Church declared by the Lord Himself before He suffered, of which the apostles were again reminded when He had been taken up from them into heaven. When our Lord stood before the High Priest, and when he said to Him, "I adjure thee, by the living God, that thou tell us whether thou be the Christ the Son of God, Jesus saith unto him, Thou hast said; nevertheless, I say unto you, Hereafter shall ye see the Son of man sitting on the right hand of power, and coming in the clouds of heaven"[2] (Matt. 26:64). Who is

---

[2] Our Lord, in this brief answer, refers to several Scriptures; besides Dan. 7:13, He alludes to Psalm 80:17, "Let thy hand be upon the man of thy right hand, upon the Son of man whom thou madest strong for thyself. So will not we go back from thee," etc. Here the Son of man, at the right hand of God, is spoken of as the only hope and deliverer for Israel.

there that cannot see how plain is the reference to the manifestation of the glory of Christ? The chief priests and scribes had not heard the discourse on the Mount of Olives, but they felt no doubt that our Lord claimed to be the person spoken of as "the Son of man" in Daniel 7, who would (He said) come forth, when He should be seen in glory by those who had rejected Him. "Ye shall see" has to do, not with the persons then addressed, but with Israel in unbelief looked at corporately.

In the revelation given to the beloved disciple in Patmos, we again find the same accompaniments of the second advent of the Lord Jesus: "Behold, He cometh with clouds; and every eye shall see Him, and they also which pierced Him; and all kindreds of the earth shall wail because of Him"[3] (Rev. 1:7); and to this promise the

---

Psalm 110:1 ("The Lord said unto my Lord, Sit thou at my right hand, until I make thine enemies thy footstool") points out the place into which the rejected Messiah should be received, until He comes forth to set His feet on those whom Jehovah will have set as His footstool, when He gives Him the commission, "Rule thou in the midst of thine enemies."

[3] It is scarcely needful to point out the use made in this passage of Zech. 12:10: I will pour upon the house of David, and upon the inhabitants of Jerusalem, the spirit of grace and of supplications: and they shall look upon me whom they have pierced, and they shall mourn for him, as one mourneth for his only son, and shall be in bitterness for him, as one that is in bitterness for his first-born." How clearly does the connection of this passage, taken with its context, show that the coming of the Lord in the clouds of heaven is that which leads to the national conversion of Israel: "In that day there shall be a fountain opened to the house of David and to the inhabitants of Jerusalem for sin and for uncleanness." Just as clearly does the use of Daniel 7, in connection with the Lord's coming, show that He shall then reign as receiving a kingdom on earth; for there are then those to whom shall be

response is, "Even so; Amen." Thus, if we see the coming of Christ spoken of in connection with judgment on persecuting Gentile powers, or in relation to Israel, when His believing people are addressed as to their hope, this event is spoken of in similar language. There is no hope set before the Church prior to the appearing of the Lord in the clouds of heaven: this is taught us in almost every way that can be conceived; because the Lord knew that our minds would be liable to the same inattention, and there would be in the Church the same dimness of apprehension, which He found in His disciples who were around Him when He was on earth. Are we looking on to this appearing of the Lord in visible glory, after iniquity and oppression have reached their height, and immediately after the unequalled tribulation, or have we formed some other hope in our minds? It is to this coming in the clouds of heaven that the apostles were directed when Jesus ascended; it is to the testimony to this coming that the Apostle John responds, "Even so; Amen."

---

given (with Him and under Him) "the kingdom and dominion, and the greatness of the kingdom under the whole heaven" (verse 27).

S. P. Tregelles

Chapter 4
Knowledge of Prophetic Details Not Necessary

It has sometimes been thought that a minute investigation of the details of Scripture prophecy is needful in order to form any judgment as to the manner in which the Scripture presents the second coming of the Lord; and thus, if prophetic details are not understood, or if there is a difficulty in the mind respecting them, the simple subject of the Lord's coming is either left as one on which no judgment is formed, or else there is an acquiescence of an indefinite kind in the opinions of someone who is supposed (perhaps truly) to be more instructed in Scripture. But while all prophetic details, if rightly learned from the Word of God, have their value in this as in other respects, so far from a knowledge of such minute points being needful as a prerequisite, a definite apprehension of the manner in which the Lord's second advent is taught in the Word of God, is the rather that which is indispensably necessary as the antecedent qualification; for thus a Christian mind may enter on the details of those prophecies which teach what shall be the future, whether of the Jews, the Gentiles, or the Church of God. This follows from that one event being the turning point in the

The Hope of Christ's Second Coming

dispensational dealing of God. If, then, we have to learn anything as to the details of revealed truth, the primary point is, how our hope—the coming of the Lord Jesus—is set before us.

For if a detailed acquaintance with prophetic expectations is needful before the Lord's coming can be understood, how would it have been possible for the apostles, or for the Lord Jesus Himself, to have taught anything on the subject? How could they have used it as [an] animating hope, leading to watchfulness, sustaining under trial, or purifying the believer? But they did so use it as a fact, the reality of which was apprehended in such a manner that the circumstances could be taught and enforced as to their moral bearings. A marked instance of this is given in the conclusion of 1 Thessalonians 4. The Apostle comforts the Thessalonian Christians concerning their departed brethren, teaching them (what they seem not to have fully known) that the whole "Church of the first-born" shall be gathered together at the coming of the Lord; the dead being raised, and the living changed. He then tells them how the Lord shall come: "The Lord himself shall descend from heaven with a shout, with the voice of the archangel, and with the trump of God: and the dead in Christ shall rise first: then we which are alive and remain shall be caught up together with them in the clouds, to meet the Lord in the air: and so shall we ever be with the Lord. Wherefore comfort one another with these words."[4] And this the most uninstructed Christian may do

---

[4] The expression "we which are alive and remain" is what the Church may ever use; it has nothing to do with individual expectancy, but it is the language of corporate hope. "We shall be changed" (1 Cor. 15:52) is of precisely the same character: that portion of the one Church which is living at

S. P. Tregelles

who simply accepts the words of the Apostle as being the truth of God. The scene presented is the very reverse of secrecy: the Lord comes with a shout; His call shall wake the dead; but besides this, the voice of the archangel shall be also heard; and, as if the notion of publicity were intended to be specially enforced, there shall be the sounding of the trump of God. This is just what Christ has promised in Matt. 24:31, when He comes with the clouds of heaven. To say that this triple sound shall not be heard by all, would be a mere addition to Holy Scripture of a kind that contradicts its testimony. We might as well say that "every eye shall see Him" means that He shall only be visible to some few. Above shall be heard the shout, the voice, and the trumpet: on earth the graves of all the sleeping family of faith shall be opened; the sleepers shall

---

any given time may use it; for so long as we are alive we do, in fact, belong to the number of the living expectants in contrast to those who have fallen asleep. To suppose that the Apostle imagined when he wrote the first epistle to the Thessalonians, that the coming of the Lord was so near that he would then be living, is to assume that before he wrote his second epistle he had received such light as to contradict his own previous teaching—a notion utterly subversive of the authority of the first epistle, and also contradictory to the teaching of that epistle itself (Chapter 5:1,2); contradictory also to the fact that he had taught the Thessalonians, when with them, some of the things which he enforces in the second epistle: "Remember ye not that when I was with you I told you these things." He must, therefore, have had all this light before he wrote his first epistle. "We," in corporate expressions, means that portion of the whole body to whom the term can apply. An Israelite will now say, "The Lord led us out of Egypt, and brought us through the Red Sea, and gave us the land which He sware unto our fathers;" but no one imagines that he applies this to himself, or to the generation of men now living.

arise: and then those living shall with them be caught up to meet the Lord in the air. This, as thus set forth, ought to be our hope. It may have been needful to teach the Thessalonians that the day of the Lord must still be waited for; that the falling away and the revelation of the man of sin had first to take place; but even these things connect themselves with the same hope; for this Head of evil is he "whom the Lord shall consume with the spirit of His mouth, and shall destroy with the brightness of His coming" (2 Thess. 2:8). "It is a righteous thing with God to recompense tribulation to them that trouble you; and to you who are troubled, rest with us, when the Lord Jesus shall be revealed" (2 Thess. 1:6,7). Thus, at the revelation of Christ from heaven, there shall be rest for His Church, and the destruction of their oppressors. The date which the Spirit gives for both is the same. The Church is called to "patience of hope," and not to mere excitement of speculative expectancy. "The Lord direct your hearts into the love of God, and into the patient waiting for Christ" (2 Thess. 3:5).

S. P. Tregelles

Chapter 5
An Interval Taught by the Lord

In the discourse of our Lord to His apostles the evening before His crucifixion (John 14-16), He contemplated His Church as being left here on this earth for a considerable period: the instruction then given for its guidance during such an interval, and the mission of the Holy Ghost, as the other Paraclete, was for the right endowment of such to live and act in the circumstances. Jesus tells them in the beginning of this discourse, what their hope should be: "I will come again and receive you unto myself, that where I am, there ye may be also" (John 14:3). So that every direction, every warning, and every promise of support, would relate to persons thus waiting. From this we may draw the instruction, that it is thus, and in no other way, that we are called to wait. One thing especially which the Lord promised to His disciples was suffering: "If the world hate you, ye know that it hated me before it hated you...if they have persecuted me, they will also persecute you" (John 15:18,20). "They shall put you out of the synagogues; yea, the time cometh that whosoever killeth you will think that he doeth God service" (John 16:2). The whole of the three chapters may be taken as containing proof after proof, not only that there would be (as we know that the facts have shown) a long interval between the departure of the Lord and His personal return, but that they were taught that such an interval would be; so that they knew that the Lord's coming could not take place until certain things had occurred, and until certain moral features of opposition between the Church and the world had displayed themselves.

Persecution is here one of the significant tokens; and this, too, had been specified particularly in Matthew 24: "Then shall they deliver you up to be afflicted, and shall kill you; and ye shall be hated of all nations for my name's sake: and then shall many be offended, and shall betray one another, and hate one another" (verses 9,10). This shall be the treatment received by the Church from without; but will all be truth and peace within its professing pale? "Many false prophets shall arise, and shall deceive many; and because iniquity shall abound, the love of many shall wax cold" (verses 11,12). In all this a course of time is distinctly marked out, as that which must elapse before Christ should come to receive His people to Himself.

In every place in which the commission to preach the Gospel is stated, it is very clear that a sufficient length of time is supposed during which it would go forth into the different spheres of testimony. "All power is given unto me in heaven and in earth; go ye therefore and teach all nations, baptizing them in the name of the Father, and of the Son, and of the Holy Ghost; teaching them to observe all things whatsoever I have commanded you: and lo, I am with you always, even unto the end of the world [age]" (Matt. 28:18–20). "Go ye into all the world, and preach the Gospel to every creature" (Mark 16:15). "Ye shall receive power after that the Holy Ghost is come upon you; and ye shall be witnesses unto me, both in Jerusalem, and in all Judaea, and in Samaria, and unto the uttermost parts of the earth" (Acts 1:8).

The Church was taught that she was called to a place of service, and also of trial: the hope of the coming of her Lord was that by which she was to be animated in the one, and sustained in the other. She knew that certain moral signs should precede that coming; she knew also that certain definite occurrences should first take place; but, resting on the word of her Lord, it was her calling to look onward, even though the interval were of necessity long. The Lord showed His grace in instructing His people by His truth. Had He held out different expectations, might it not have seemed as if He had indeed given a hope that must make ashamed?

THE HOPE OF CHRIST'S SECOND COMING

S. P. Tregelles

Chapter 6
Apostolic Testimony

Five of the Apostles of the Lord Jesus Christ have left in their epistles instruction for the Church in all ages. Amongst other subjects of which they all treat, more or less, is that of the coming of the Lord, and the facts or moral features which precede that event. Thus the Apostle John (1 John 2:18) says, "Little children, it is the last time; and as ye have heard that Antichrist shall come, even now are there many Antichrists; whereby we know it is the last time." This one passage shows us that the Church had then been taught concerning the coming of Antichrist; that the Apostle knew that they had received this teaching; and that it was right that Christians should understand that this is a thing that concerns the Church: in the beginning of the next chapter he speaks of the hope of our being like Christ when He shall be manifested: that is our hope; and because it is our hope, we may contemplate the rise and working of Antichrist, or of anything else that the Scripture says shall take place first. Opposers of simple Scripture teaching sometimes ask, "For which are you waiting, Christ or Antichrist?" The answer might be, "Which does the Apostle teach us shall be first, the coming of Antichrist, or the revelation of Christ?" for if we take these things in their Scriptural order, we shall not go wrong. We wait for Christ, and therefore we can take heed to the warnings concerning the rise of Antichrist; "These things have I written unto you concerning them that seduce you;" and we can seek to be so instructed from God's Word as not to be entangled with the snares of the many Antichrists, or those of Antichrist himself, the denier of the Father and the Son. Will any one, with the Scripture before him, say that he there learns that the rise of Antichrist shall not precede the coming of Christ? Will he say that the learnings of the inspired Apostle have no application?

The Apostle James (Chapter 5) speaks of the evil characteristics of "the last days;" in contrast to which he says, "Be patient, therefore, brethren, unto the coming of the Lord. Behold, the husbandman waiteth for the precious fruit of the earth, and hath long patience for it, until he receive the early and the latter rain. Be ye also patient, stablish your hearts; for the coming of the Lord draweth nigh." (James 5:7,8.) This, then, shows what the kind of waiting for the Lord's coming was which this Apostle taught: it was that in which "long patience" was needed. The expression, "the coming of the Lord draweth nigh," is not one to be measured by mere interval of time, but rather with the intelligence of its absolute certainty, even though the intervening period might seem great.[5]

---

[5] We also learn in the Epistle of James how to act and to speak in relation to present plans. In reproving those who plan what they will do, he tells them that what they ought to say is, "If the Lord will, we shall live, and do this or that" (James 4:15). He does not make instantaneous looking for the coming of the Lord the reason why such things should not be said or done. He does not say (as some now do), in speaking of things presently before them, "Unless the Lord come first."

It was not only revealed to the Apostle Paul that there would be evil days, both in the Church and in the world, before Christ's second advent, but he was also inspired by the Holy Ghost to communicate this as being [a] profitable and needful warning. Not only do we find the prophetic statements in the Thessalonians to this effect, but also in other places. For instance: "Now the Spirit speaketh expressly that in the latter times some shall depart from the faith, giving heed to seducing spirits and doctrines of devils," etc. (1 Tim. 4:1). Until these things had been accomplished, the coming of the Lord could not take place. So, too, in the Second Epistle to Timothy, containing, as it does, what may be called the dying testimony of the Apostle: "This know also, that in the last days perilous times shall come" (2 Tim. 3:1). "Evil men and seducers shall wax worse and worse, deceiving and being deceived" (2 Tim. 3:13). "The time will come when they will not endure sound doctrine; but after their own lusts shall they heap to themselves teachers, having itching ears; and they shall turn away their ears from the truth, and shall be turned unto fables" (2 Tim. 4:3,4). The servant of the Lord, in contrast to all this, had to look to the crown of life, which the Lord, the righteous Judge, shall give in that day unto all that love His appearing. Thus the hope of the Lord's coming is in perfect harmony with the knowledge of intervening events. Indeed, if this had not been the case, not a single future occurrence, not a single direction which involves the knowledge of interval of time, could the Lord have given to His people. If a moral effect were thus to be wrought, it would be by the withholding of truth, and not by its communication. All the teaching of St. Paul's epistles for the continuous guidance of the Church, assumes, as an admitted truth,

The Hope of Christ's Second Coming

that there would be those living on the earth, prior to the Lord's coming, who should be so guided.

Jude, in his one short epistle, gives a solemn testimony as to the condition in which the coming of the Lord (as prophesied of old by Enoch) should find the world and the Church. He does not communicate these things in order to discourage Christians, but rather that they might see proof of the faithfulness of God, and of the mercy of His warnings: "But, beloved, remember the words which were spoken before of the Apostles of our Lord Jesus Christ; how that they told you that there should be mockers in the last time, who should walk after their own ungodly lusts." (verses 17,18.)

The Lord Jesus had declared to Peter "by what death he should glorify God" (John 21:19): thus that Apostle himself knew, and other Christians also knew, that the coming of the Lord could not take place until after he had thus suffered martyrdom. If our hope of the second advent be the same as theirs, we may at once see that absolute certainty of previous events does not interfere with it. Now the Apostle Peter was desirous that the hope of those coming after him should be the same as that which he had himself cherished and taught. He not only thought it meet while in this tabernacle to stir up believers by putting them in remembrance, but he says, in relation to his approaching death, which the Lord had shown him. "Moreover, I will endeavour that ye may be able after my decease to have these things always in remembrance" (2 Peter 1:15). The scene on the Mount of Transfiguration had been a showing forth of the glory of Christ at His coming, and to this Peter directed the minds of Christians, teaching them that they ought to give heed to the prophetic word while waiting for the dawning of the day. What, then, were Christians to expect during the interval before the coming of Christ? "There shall be false teachers among you, who privily shall bring in damnable heresies, even denying the Lord that bought them, and bring upon themselves swift destruction: and many shall follow their pernicious ways, by reason of whom the way of truth shall be evil spoken of;" and so on throughout the second chapter. These were to be the expectations of those whose hope was like that of the Church as then taught. In warning of the heed which should be paid to the words spoken before by the holy prophets, and to the commandments of apostles, he draws their attention to one special point: "Knowing this first, that there shall come in the last days scoffers walking after their own lusts, and saying, Where is the promise of His coming; for since the fathers fell asleep, all things continue as they were from the beginning of the creation?" (2 Peter 3:3,4). Thus the moral power of the hope of the coming of Christ was not marred in the apostles' days from their possessing a certain knowledge of events that would intervene: the apostles authoritatively taught this doctrine as being of importance to the Church; and if any doctrine of the second advent is now taught which cannot be held with such knowledge of events, or which would deny that such knowledge could be held compatibly with the maintenance of the hope, then we may be sure that such doctrine is not in accordance with Holy Scripture, and that, in fact, it sets aside its solemn teaching. The promise of His coming must be held as the promise was made, and not in some manner wholly different. At the Pentecostal preaching of the Gospel, the apostles of the Lord well knew that they were not setting forth that which was to bring in universal blessing; they knew that although the promise of the return of the Lord Jesus to reign was a portion of their testimony, it would not be as yet; and thus part of the

The Hope of Christ's Second Coming

exhortation of Peter was founded on that knowledge: "Save yourselves from this untoward generation" (Acts 2:40). Thus a definite interval was part of the original doctrine.

S. P. Tregelles

Chapter 7
The Book of Revelation and The First Resurrection

There are some who appear to shrink from using any testimony from the Book of Revelation, either from mistrusting their ability to comprehend any part of it, or else from alarm at the additions to Holy Scripture found in some of the professed expositions. But when the Book of Revelation touches on common points of truth, every believer who knows what the Cross of Christ has wrought, may feel in his soul a response as to such things at least. Thus the thanksgiving, "Unto Him that loved us, and washed us from our sins in His own blood.... To Him be glory and dominion for ever and ever" (Rev. 1:5,6), is one to which every believer can respond.[6] So, too, in the

---

[6] "Although the object of this paper is not critical, yet I may point out the ancient reading in Rev. 22:14: μακάριοι οἱ πλύνοντες τὰς στολὰς αὐτῶν, "Blessed are they that wash their robes," instead of [the rendering] μακ. οἱ ποιοῦντες τὰς ἐντολὰς αὐτοῦ, "Blessed are they that do His commandments," of the common and recent text. This ancient reading (confirmed by the recently discovered *Codex Sinaiticus*) is one which has refreshed many a believing heart;

35

The Hope of Christ's Second Coming

heavenly scene in Chapter 5, where "Thou art worthy" is the address to the Lamb once slain, on the ground of the redemption wrought out in His blood. So, too, in Chapter 7, where the great multitude appear before the throne: "These are they which came out of great tribulation, and have washed their robes, and made them white in the blood of the Lamb; therefore are they before the throne of God," etc. Whatever difficulty there may be in understanding Chapter 12, we seem to find in verse 11 a key-note to connect us with those there spoken of: "And they overcame him by the blood of the Lamb, and by the word of their testimony, and they loved not their lives unto the death:" thus, whoever they are, it is the blood of the same Saviour whom we know which is the ground of their victory. Whatever the Revelation teaches as to redemption and its results has an identity with what we know.

---

for while it is true that those who are accepted in grace are doers of His commandments, yet the ground of all blessing is the blood of the Lamb that was shed, and this it is that entitles those whose garments are washed, to enter into the holy city above. To prevent all misconception, it is right to state that, although the ancient reading in Rev. 1:5 (quoted above) is τῷ ἀγαπῶντι ἡμᾶς καὶ λύσαντι ἡμᾶς, "to Him that loveth us and freed us" (instead of [the rendering] τῷ ἀγαπήσαντι ἡμᾶς καὶ λούσαντι ἡμᾶς) "from our sins in His own blood," yet no part of the doctrine of redemption by blood is lost: we are only thrown back from the present application of the blood to us, to the far deeper thing, its having been given as the availing price of redemption. The blood was the λύτρον given once for all. The first use that we have of λύω relates to deliverance by price paid.

> ὁ γὰρ ἦλθε θοὰs ἐπὶ νηas 'Αχαιῶν
> λυσόμενόs τε θύγατρα φέρων τ' ἀπερείσι' ἄποινα.

S. P. Tregelles

But it is not only the mention of the blood of the Lamb which connects this book with our familiar thoughts; for where it speaks of resurrection, it tells us of one of the fundamental verities of our faith, and one which may be the more illustrated from what we here find.

In Revelation 20 we read of "the first resurrection." The whole scene is thus described: "I saw thrones, and they sat upon them; and judgment was given unto them; and I saw the souls of them that were beheaded for the witness of Jesus, and for the Word of God, and [those] which had not worshipped the beast, neither his image, neither had received his mark upon their foreheads or in their hands; and they lived and reigned with Christ a thousand years. (But the rest of the dead lived not again until the thousand years were finished.) This is the first resurrection. Blessed and holy is he that hath part in the first resurrection: on such the second death hath no power, but they shall be priests of God and of Christ, and shall reign with Him a thousand years." This is not only a vision, but also an explanation. John is taught what the thrones with certain sitting upon them meant. They are the faithful in Christ in general (i.e. the whole family of faith from Abel onward), and one special class, those suffering for the witness of Jesus; and the glory given to them is explained to be the first resurrection. This is in full accordance with other Scriptures; for instance, 1 Cor. 15:23, where the order of the resurrection is taught: "Every man in his own order: Christ the first-fruits; afterward (i.e. next in order), they that are Christ's at His coming." The concluding part of 1 Thessalonians 4 equally connects the resurrection of the Church with the coming of Christ, so that there can be no resurrection of the saints till then. And so in this passage in Revelation 20; for the narrative, both in vision and in explanation, runs

The Hope of Christ's Second Coming

on from the time when He whose "name is called the Word of God" is seen on the White Horse, when the beast and the kings of the earth and their armies are gathered to make war with Him, and when destruction falls upon them: then it is that those recently suffering under the persecuting power of this beast are sharers in the first resurrection. Until the beast and his persecution are destroyed together, there can be no first resurrection.

Thus, in the teaching of Christ Himself, and of His apostles, the one object before the souls of believers is His own personal coming in manifested glory. This is our hope; for then, in body and in spirit, we shall share His glory. That coming will bring destruction on Gentile power then in its height of blasphemy and persecution: then will Israel look on Him whom they pierced and mourn for Him: then shall the spirit of grace and supplications be poured on them, and then shall they know the fountain for sin and for uncleanness to be opened for them.

If we receive this hope, as taught us from the Word of God, we must also see that it is given us to strengthen and sustain during the intervening time; not as telling us that there is no such interval (for God can only teach truth), but as sustaining us through it; so that while we learn of false teachers and evil in the Church, and while we know much of the course of sin and its fruits in the world, we have before us the brightness of the morning to sustain during the darkness of the night.

The ancient prophecies of universal blessing must have their full accomplishment, but that can never be till the Lord takes the dominion manifestly into His own hand. During this dispensation the broad way is thronged by the many, while but few find the narrow; all that will live godly in Christ Jesus must expect persecution, at least in principle. Christ's people shall be hated of all nations for His name's sake. But when the Lord comes, not only shall the Church of the first-born enter into heavenly blessing, both in body and in spirit, but restored and believing Israel shall know God's faithfulness to them, and then shall the nations be blessed under the rule of Christ.

THE HOPE OF CHRIST'S SECOND COMING

S. P. Tregelles

Chapter 8
The 'Secret Rapture' Explained

But there is a very different theory of the coming of the Lord as the hope of His Church, which many teach, and which many more receive, as though it were unquestioned truth.

It is said that there shall be a secret coming of the Lord Jesus Christ; that at this secret coming His believing people who are in their graves shall be raised, and the living changed, and that a secret rapture of the Church shall then take place; that this secret coming and secret rapture are our hope, and not the manifested appearing of Christ in the clouds of heaven.

It is said that after this secret removal of the Church, the full manifestation of human evil, for some years at least, will take place, during which time shall be the display of the power of Antichrist, the persecutions foretold in the Revelation, the extreme trials of Israel, the unequalled tribulation; and that at the end of this will be the manifestation of Christ visibly coming with His Church in the cloud of glory.

This is the doctrine of the secret coming of Christ, which many now preach as if it were the acknowledged truth of God, instead of its being (as is really the case) that which at every point would require proof from Scripture.

The Hope of Christ's Second Coming

But not only is this doctrine of the coming of Christ not taught in the Word of God, but if, in what has been previously said, there is any point of truth, then this whole system stands in distinct contradiction of what the Scripture reveals. It is refuted by whatever speaks of the Lord's coming in the clouds of heaven when every eye shall see Him, as being our hope; but it was to this that the beloved Apostle responded, "Even so, Amen": by whatever speaks of events for which the people of Christ are to watch and wait, and for their right acting in which they have received instruction—by whatever tells us of the last power of evil being destroyed by the Lord at His coming, and not before—and by whatever speaks of the first resurrection occurring after the last anti-Christian persecution, and not before. It is likewise contradicted by specific and individual Scriptures, which, in simple testimony or in legitimate deduction, would be conclusive to a mind subject to God's Word.

S. P. Tregelles

Chapter 9
The 'Secret Rapture': Its Origin

When a new doctrine is taught as if it were a revealed truth, it behooves every Christian to inquire on what Scripture testimony it rests; and unless this is satisfactorily set forth, what is taught ought not to be accepted. This will apply very definitely to the system of the secret rapture and secret coming. When the hope of our Lord's second advent was revived as a point of definite teaching, when it was seen that until that day the ancient promises of blessing would not be fulfilled, there were those who thought of this one point of prophecy almost exclusively: if they turned at all to prophetic detail, it was with a kind of supposition that everything had been accomplished that was needful to introduce that day. They knew that the apostles had taught intervening events, the corruption that should take place in the Church from false teachers, etc.; they knew that the knowledge of such truths had once been a right thing, and that it had not been inconsistent with the hope of the coming of Christ; but now there was a kind of supposition that such prophecies had been exhausted, and that there might be a kind of momentary expectation of the Lord's appearing. This supposition was, apparently, not then connected with the belief in a secret coming or a secret rapture.

The Hope of Christ's Second Coming

But when a closer study of prophecy had led to the conviction that many things remained unaccomplished, such as must precede the reign of Christ, there was an unwillingness to give up the opinions previously conceived—there was an endeavor to hold the prophetic detail without giving up the thought of the coming of Christ, apart from the possibility that any intervening events could be part of our expectation. This led to the adoption of theories by which definite points of revelation were explained away; and for the support of which it became needful to maintain that the moral power of the hope of the Lord's coming is lost, if any intervening event, any sign, is supposed to be a portion of truth. This, if deliberately held, would show that the apostles, and the Apostolic Church, who, as a fact, knew of certain intervening events, did not so hold the hope as to apprehend it in its moral power.

The tone of thought thus arrived at was quite different from that which recognized that intervening events had once been known, but in which it was assumed that they were now exhausted.

But still it seems as if it were some time before a secret advent of the Lord and a secret rapture of the Church had a definite and systematic place. It was rather as if the coming of Christ had been divided into two parts: indeed, there were those then who said that He would appear in glory, and when He had taken the Church He would cease to be seen until He came to crush the powers of evil, and then reign. This would, however, be virtually a second and third coming; it would err in the fact of addition to Holy Scripture, as well as in that of contradiction to its testimony.

S. P. Tregelles

But when the theory of a secret coming of Christ was first brought forward (about the year 1832),[7] it was adopted with eagerness: it suited certain preconceived opinions, and it was accepted by some as that which harmonized contradictory thoughts. There should,

---

[7] I am not aware that there was any definite teaching that there would be a secret rapture of the Church at a secret coming, until this was given forth as an "utterance" in Mr. Irving's Church, from what was there received as being the voice of the Spirit. But whether any one ever asserted such a thing or not, it was from that supposed revelation that the modern doctrine and the modern phraseology respecting it arose. It came not from Holy Scripture, but from that which falsely pretended to be the Spirit of God, while not owning the true doctrine of our Lord's incarnation in the same flesh and blood as His brethren, but without taint of sin. After the opinion of a secret advent had been adopted, many expressions in older writers were regarded as supporting it; in which, however, the word "secret" does not mean unperceived or unknown, but simply secret in point of time. Thus in a passage of Milinan—

"Even thus amidst thy pride and luxury,
O! Earth, shall this last coming burst on thee,
That secret coming of the Son of man;
When all the cherub-throning clouds shall shine,
Irradiate with His bright advancing sign,
When the great Husbandman shall wave His fan," etc.

The third line was taken up as if it taught the new doctrine of this secret coming; whereas the whole passage (even if it had any theological value) teaches a coming in power, glory, and publicity, in contrast to that which is private: so, too, as to other writers, whose words were sometimes used.

Sometimes from a hymn being altered, writers appear to set forth a secret rapture of which they had never heard, or against which they have protested.

however, have been a previous point determined, whether such contradictory thoughts, or any of them, rested on the sure warrant of God's written Word.

Thus the doctrine held and taught by many is, that believers are concerned not with a public and manifested coming of Christ in the clouds of heaven with power and great glory—not with His appearing when every eye shall see Him, and when He shall sever the wicked from among the just, but with a secret or private coming, when the dead saints shall be secretly raised, the living changed, and both caught up to meet the Lord in the air—that the shout, the voice of the archangel, and the trump of God, do not indicate anything of publicity, for the ear of faith alone shall hear them—that the Church shall meet the Lord, not at His visible coming, but in order to remain with Him, at least for years, before His manifested advent—that after this secret coming there shall be in the earth a full power of evil put forth amongst both Jews and Gentiles that there shall be a time of unequalled tribulation and great spiritual perils (with which the Church has nothing to do) and that this condition of things shall end by the manifest coming of the Lord.[8]

---

[8] In 1863, I heard it publicly and definitely maintained, that the secret coming is the second coming promised in Scripture, and that the manifest appearing of our Lord is His third coming. Many seem to think this who do not say so in definite words. But a third coming is something very different from His coming again.

S. P. Tregelles

Chapter 10
The Jewish 'Waste-paper Basket'

But if things are so, to whom would the Scriptures apply which give warning of perilous times? To whom could signs be given? This consideration has led to the Jewish interpretation of Scripture. Whatever has been felt to be a difficulty has been set aside by saying that it is "Jewish;" and that one word has been deemed to be quite enough to show that it has nothing to do with the Church. On this principle the application of very much of the New Testament has been avoided. If Jewish circumstances of any kind are found in a passage, or if the persons addressed were Jews by nation, these particulars have been relied on as showing that it does not apply to the Church. But it must ever be borne in mind that, however differing in external circumstances, the Church is one body, dwelt in by one Spirit: the Jew and the Gentile, alike brought near to God by the blood of Christ, are one in Him; so that Jewish circumstances or Gentile circumstances do not affect the essential unity. The apostles were all of them Jews; nevertheless, it is on the twelve stones inscribed with their twelve names that the heavenly city is builded. It is quite true that there are Scriptures which treat simply of hopes and promises for Israel; these, too, shall be accomplished fully; but the acknowledgment that some portions of Holy Writ are such, does not at all warrant the

The Hope of Christ's Second Coming

avoidance of the force of any part of the Christian Scriptures. It is easy to see who are addressed—whenever the Lord or an inspired Apostle speaks to believers, whether Jews or Gentiles, they are treated as part of the one Church. There are in the New Testament personal addresses, corporate addresses, and teaching which might have to do with mere temporary or local circumstances. Just so do we find in the Pentateuch directions to Moses as an individual, precepts for guidance while in the desert, and ordinances to be obeyed in the land. There is no difficulty in distinguishing these things, unless, indeed, we choose to raise it for ourselves.

If the application of the Jewish theory of interpretation of definite New Testament prophecies be carefully examined, it will be found to refute itself; for it will give to Jews as Jews what most certainly belongs to the Church of Christ, and it will assume that Jews in their unbelief are found using the authority of the Lord Jesus Christ as a teacher. Thus, when Matthew 24 has been used as teaching how we are to expect the Lord, it has been repeatedly said that it is entirely "Jewish." Let this be granted. But what then? Who are to use it, or to take heed to its warnings? No one can acknowledge Jesus there as a teacher without owning Him as the Christ: "Many shall come in my name, saying, I am Christ, and shall deceive many" (Matt. 24:5). The persons who will use the warnings, and who will expect the manifest appearing of Christ, as here spoken of, must be believers in His divine mission, and thus their profession must simply be that of believers in His name; in other words, they must be a part of the Church of the first-born, to which all belong who now accept the Lord Jesus as He is set forth by God.

An undefined term becomes an easy mode of explaining away distinct statements which cannot be reconciled to a theory; because in this manner no meaning whatever is assigned to the passages whose testimony has to be avoided. This has been the case with the word "Jewish" in connection with the Scriptures which teach the manifest appearing of the Lord in glory. In this manner the three first Gospels have been called Jewish, whenever any portion of their teaching was felt as a difficulty. So, too, the Epistle to the Hebrews, and those of James and Peter. And yet how very much of the most blessed teaching for the Church is contained in these so-called Jewish portions of the New Testament.

In order to avoid applications of certain Scriptures to us, doctrines have been called Jewish also: thus it has been said that Covenant, Priesthood, and Mediation, are altogether Jewish. To this it has been added that the Church, "the body of Christ," stands altogether above everything of the kind; even "above dispensation" (whatever this may mean). It would have been difficult to suppose that these opinions would have found any acceptance, if such were not the known fact. What if the expression the New Testament, or Covenant, stands in opposition to the Old Covenant with Israel? It does not make the New Covenant a merely Jewish thing. Just as the Lord Jesus said the night before He suffered, "This is my blood of the New Testament which is shed for many for the remission of sins" (Matt. 26:28); so, also, did the Apostle Paul teach as parts of His words, and as applied to converted Gentiles, "This cup is the New Testament in my blood" (1 Cor. 11:25).[9] We might as well say that "the

---

[9] I have heard it maintained that the Lord's Supper, as instituted and as recorded in the Gospels, is so simply "Jewish," that the command, "This do in remembrance of me," would be no warrant to us for observing it, if the Apostle Paul had not received of the Lord that which also he

remission of sins" is Jewish, and that the shedding of the blood of Christ is Jewish: we might as well affirm that these have no relation to us, as explain away Covenant and its connected truths. (See Appendix A.)

---

delivered to the Corinthians, and to other Churches gathered from among the Gentiles! What is this but building up a new wall of partition against believers who are Jews by nature?

S. P. Tregelles

Chapter 11
Analogy Is Not Necessarily Proof

When proofs have been asked for the doctrine of the secret advent and secret removal of the Church, certain supposed analogies have been sometimes presented instead, which were thought to bear on the subject. But as analogy is a resemblance of relations, it is needful that the facts should be first known and demonstrated instead of their being merely supposed. It has been asked if the crossing of Jordan by the children of Israel was not a thing known to them only at the time, and not heard of by the Canaanites till afterwards? Whether Elijah is not to be taken as a type of the Church, and Elisha as that of "the Jewish remnant"? Whether the ascension of the Lord from the Mount of Olives, seen by the disciples only, does not intimate a second advent only to be known by the Church? This last consideration, if it had any force, might seem to avoid the expectation of any coming of the Lord in the clouds of heaven in manifested glory. But not only are supposed analogies wholly insufficient to prove facts, but they are shown to be groundless, so soon as they are seen to be in opposition to any demonstrated point. When a truth has been proved from Scripture, then analogies may illustrate it; but they never can be the ground on which an elaborate system of teaching can be based. The teachers of the secret coming have first to show that the Word of God sets forth such a doctrine, and that the Church is not called on to look for the coming of her Savior in the clouds of heaven, when every eye shall see Him.

A negative endeavor has been made to prove the secret removal of the Church. It has been said, that "in certain Scriptures, which speak of future events, no mention is made of the Church being on earth; therefore, of course, it has been removed in the manner in which we teach." But in this it is assumed, that persons spoken of in any Scriptures referred to are not the Church, or part of the Church; secondly, the absence of all mention of the Church would not prove that it had been removed by a secret rapture; for, as this secret transaction is not mentioned in Scripture, it is a mere assumption of the point to be proved, to say that a silence respecting the Church at a particular time is a decisive reference to it. (See Appendix B.)

We might as well argue, as certain Romanists have done, that when we are told in Acts 12:17, that Peter "went into another place," he went to Rome to establish his See; asking (as they do), if he did not go to Rome, where else did he go? and, if this cannot be answered, then assuming that it must teach that he then commenced his (supposed) primacy of twenty-five years in that city.[10] To

---

[10] When questions were raised in the Jewish schools, by the Sadducean party apparently, as to where Daniel was when his companions refused to worship the image of Nebuchadnezzar and were, in consequence, cast into the burning fiery furnace, a reply was given (on the principle, apparently, of answering a fool according to his folly), "He was sent to Alexandria to purchase swine;" when the questioners treated this as wholly irrelevant, they were told to prove the negative, and if they

connect a negative fact with a supposition, does not add to the probability of the latter.

Differences of names and designations do not prove differences of classes; and this is especially the case when there is some figurative expression used, or some collective term for a corporate body. Thus, in Eph. 1:22,23, the Church is Christ's "body," and, in the same epistle (Eph. 5:25–32), it is His spouse, the bride for whom He gave Himself, "that He might sanctify and cleanse it with the washing of water by the word, that He might present it to himself a glorious Church." The same epistle speaks of believers as "saints" and "faithful in Christ Jesus" (Eph. 1:1), and yet the children of God may be equally truly reminded that they are servants of a Master in heaven (Eph. 6:8). It is from the assumption that different terms or different figures must denote different bodies of persons, instead of different relations of the same persons, that the opinion has been framed of the Church's exclusion from various Scriptures.

Thus, when the Revelation is said to be given "to show unto His servants things which must shortly come to pass," it has been said that the term "servants" shows that it is not intended for us, who are not servants, but sons of God, and brethren of Christ. This argument has been used by those who would evade the testimony of this book. But have such never read how the apostles of the Lord use and claim the term servant as pertaining to themselves?

"Paul, a servant of Jesus Christ, called to be an apostle" (Rom. 1:1).

"James, a servant of God, and of the Lord Jesus Christ" (James 1:1).

---

could not show to what other place he was gone, to admit that he had been sent to Alexandria.

The Hope of Christ's Second Coming

"Simon Peter, a servant and an apostle of Jesus Christ" (2 Peter 1:1).

"Jude, the servant of Jesus Christ" (Jude 1).

And Christ sent the Revelation itself "unto His servant John" (1:1); who also is addressed by the angel, "I am thy fellow servant" (Rev. 22:9).

Whoever, then, thinks of taking some essentially higher standing than that of those who in privilege are sons, but who can rejoice in being also servants, shows that his thoughts on this subject have not been formed from the teaching of the Word of God.

S. P. Tregelles

Chapter 12
1 Corinthians 15:51-54 and Isaiah 25:7-8 Compared

There are very few leading truths in Scripture which are based upon one passage merely, or upon teaching in one form: this is a gracious provision for meeting minds variously constituted as to their habits and ability of attention; those who do not feel at once the force of one kind of proof, are sometimes struck with the pointedness of another: also, there are not a few who feel the conclusiveness of a legitimate and necessary inference even more than they do that of a direct statement.

The Apostle Paul, in teaching the Corinthians the hope of the resurrection of the saints, says, "Behold, I show you a mystery; we shall not all sleep, but we shall all be changed, in a moment, in the twinkling of an eye, at the last trump: for the trumpet shall sound, and the dead shall be raised incorruptible, and we shall be changed....So when this corruptible shall have put on incorruption, and this mortal shall have put on immortality, THEN shall be brought to pass the saying that is written, Death is swallowed up in victory" (1 Cor. 15: 51–54). Where is this saying written? In Isaiah 25, in the midst of the predictions of the blessing of restored Israel, when the

The Hope of Christ's Second Coming

Lord "shall reign in mount Zion, and in Jerusalem, and before His ancients gloriously;" then "He will destroy in this mountain the face of the covering cast over all people, and the vail that is spread over all nations. He will swallow up death in victory; and the Lord God shall wipe away tears from off all faces; and the rebuke of His people shall He take away from off all the earth: for the Lord hath spoken it" (Isa. 25:7,8).

Thus it is a plain fact of revelation, that at the time of Israel's restored blessing, and not at a period (perhaps considerably) previous, shall the resurrection take place of "those who are Christ's at His coming." The Spirit of God has given us His own note of time through the combined testimony of the prophet and the apostle. There can be no coming of the Lord (much more no secret coming) until He appears for the accomplishment of His promises to His ancient people Israel. "When the Lord shall build up Zion, He shall appear in His glory" (Psalm 102:16). Any hope of a previous resurrection must be based, not on Scripture teaching, but upon some thought which has been formed in contradiction to revealed truth.

This portion of Isaiah speaks, a little farther on, of a resurrection at this time: "Thy dead men shall live" [that is, the believing dead of Israel, the Old Testament saints]; "they shall arise my dead body" [this is the literal force of the words; Messiah owns His relation to them; He speaks of them as united to Himself]. "Awake and sing, ye that dwell in dust: for thy dew is as the dew of herbs, and the earth shall cast out the dead" (Isa. 26:19).

S. P. Tregelles

Chapter 13
Tribulation Arguments Reconsidered

Lord Jesus gives a warning of an unequalled tribulation which shall immediately precede His coming in glory: "Then shall be great tribulation, such as was not since the beginning of the world to this time, no, nor ever shall be. And except those days should be shortened, there should no flesh be saved: but for the elect's sake those days shall be shortened....Immediately after the tribulation of those days shall the sun be darkened, and the moon shall not give her light, and the stars shall fall from heaven, and the powers of the heavens shall be shaken: and then shall appear the sign of the Son of Man in heaven, and then shall all the tribes of the earth mourn, and they shall see the Son of Man coming in the clouds of heaven with power and great glory" (Matt. 24:21–30). Some have said, "What a fearful prospect it is if the Church shall be in this tribulation! Can we suppose it possible that the Lord can permit any part of this suffering to fall on His redeemed and believing people? Is it not more fitting, more in accordance with His dealings in grace towards them, that they should be removed to be with Him before this trouble sets in?" And thus any theory is judged admissible which shall exclude the Church from sharing at all in this suffering, or from being on earth at the time. But we cannot draw conclusions in this transcendental manner. Thus Peter argued and spoke when his Master foretold "that He must go to Jerusalem, and suffer many things of the elders and chief priests and scribes, and be killed, and be raised again the third day." It was nature, and not spirituality, that led him to think thus of the sufferings of his Lord, rather than of the promise of His resurrection: "Be it far from thee, Lord; this shall not be unto thee" (Matt. 16:22). Should not our Lord's rebuke to Peter check all such reasonings? especially, too, when He speaks of His followers taking up their cross, losing their lives, but having before them the promise that the "Son of Man shall come in the glory of His Father?" We can never set our opinion of what is fitting in opposition to any direct statement of the Lord.

But is suffering and trial so strange a lot for the people of Christ? "These things have I spoken unto you, that in Me ye might have peace. In the world ye shall have tribulation: but be of good cheer; I have overcome the world" (John 16:33). How continually did apostles teach "that we must through much tribulation enter into the kingdom of God" (Acts 14:22)? "No man should be moved by these afflictions: for yourselves know that we are appointed thereunto. For verily, when we were with you, we told you before that we should suffer tribulation, even as it came to pass, and ye know" (1 Thess. 3:3,4). If, then, certain tribulations are to be expected as the common experience of the faithful servants of Christ, why should it seem strange that they should be instructed respecting the great and final tribulation? Why should it be thought that they must previously be taken away?

"What are these that are arrayed in white robes, and whence came they? These are they which came out of great tribulation, and have washed their robes and made them white in the blood of the Lamb: therefore are they before the throne of God, and serve Him day and night in His temple" (Rev. 7:13–15). These are "a great multitude, which no man can number, of all nations, and kindreds, and people, and tongues,"[11] whom John saw standing "before the throne and before the Lamb, clothed with white robes, and palms in their hands."

Thus the gathered assembly of those whose robes have been washed and made white in the blood of atonement, are set forth as those who have passed through great tribulation: it is so spoken of as their characteristic, that it seems as if the last scene on earth, in which they had been regarded, was one marked by tribulation.

It is said that, if the unequalled tribulation is an affliction for Israel and a punishment for the Gentile, how can the Church be in it? In this inquiry, two fallacies are assumed: First, that this tribulation is part of the

---

[11] It may illustrate some points of the Jewish system of interpretation, when I mention that I have heard it gravely maintained, that this great multitude were all Jews: not persons of, or belonging to all nations, but Jews who had been scattered amongst all nations. The use of words seems vain if it be legitimate thus to pervert them. It is not too much to call this trifling with Holy Scripture. I have also heard it taught that this is not an heavenly, but an earthly scene: that they stand on earth before the throne of God. If so, how could even the Spirit of God himself (I desire to speak reverently) find words to describe what is heavenly?

In some more recent statements, these are said to be a peculiar class, who stand in contrast to the Church; we "are washed," but these (it is said) "wash their own robes." When advocates of a system support it by such perversions, it shows that they at least lack better arguments; and that they, and all who receive their teaching, value the "secret coming" system, more than they do the doctrines of grace; for they invalidate the latter to maintain the former.

outpouring of judgment; and second, that the Church, while in the world, is exempted from part of the suffering which falls on men or on nations. For believers there is no penal suffering, because Christ in life and in death endured for His people all that is penal: any disciplinary sorrow on Israel or on the nations before Christ comes, has, in part at least, a corrective character; it ought to lead to repentance; and from this the last tribulation, though of a very special kind, is not to be excepted.[12]

But in this last tribulation, Christ is very mindful of His people: "for the elect's sake, those days shall be shortened;" and; besides this, they are warned of that time, in order that they may at once flee away from the scene of suffering. Those who believe that these warnings are intended for Christians, may, by obeying the word of the Lord, be locally removed from the fierceness of the trial; those who think such warnings are not for them, of course, cannot do this; they neglect the light which God has given them. (See Appendix C.)

Thus the Lord desires that His people should be enabled to endure; that in obedience to Him, they should

---

[12] Some who saw that the company of the redeemed in Revelation 7 are indeed the Church, and who yet would not admit that the Church can be in the special tribulation, rashly cut the knot by asserting that this company were not in the tribulation at all; "they came out of great tribulation" (verse 14) meant, according to such teachers, that they came away from it, so as not to have been in it! This they said was the force of the preposition ἐκ here. If this were true, then Colossians 1:18, where our Lord is called "the first-born (ἐκ) from the dead," would teach that He never died at all, instead of the direct contrary. If it be allowable thus to wrest words, can Almighty God himself give an unequivocal revelation of truth in human language?

S. P. Tregelles

watch the coming on of this tribulation, and that they should know that, however they may in part be sharers in it, His own coming is to follow at once.

THE HOPE OF CHRIST'S SECOND COMING

S. P. Tregelles

Chapter 14
The Double: 'Two Jewish Remnants'

So evident is it that believers in Christ are contemplated as those who shall use the warnings connected with the manifest appearing of our Lord, that many who clung tenaciously to the opinion of a secret advent and a secret rapture, and who styled everything of an opposite teaching in Scripture "Jewish," extended their theory by some remarkable additions. For a considerable time they were content to apply indefinitely to "the Jewish remnant" those parts of the New Testament which do not consist with the supposition that our Lord may come at any moment; but at length they saw that "the Jewish remnant" seemed to be, in some passages especially of the Old Testament, persons who do not own Jesus as the Christ until they see Him in glory; and that some other passages which they would not admit to be applicable to the Church, incontestably set forth persons who own the Lord Jesus before His coming in glory.

Hence arose a theory of two Jewish remnants: but neither of them part of "the Church," at least not the Church of this dispensation. It was said that after the secret rapture of the Church, a certain testimony would go forth to Israel; that by this many would be converted; some said to full faith in Christ, and others said to partial;

The Hope of Christ's Second Coming

and that this remnant would go through the unequalled tribulation, and would use the Scriptures which bear on it. It was said by those who held that this remnant would be true believers, that at the manifestation of Christ they would be taken up to a place of heavenly blessedness, whilst those of them who had been cut off by persecution would be raised from the dead: that this raised and changed body of persons should share in the full glory of "the Church" was afterwards denied by those who divided the saved into classes, making the Church, as such, to extend only from Pentecost (or as some said from the martyrdom of Stephen) until the secret rapture.

Such was "the remnant" to whom these teachers applied (with various modifications) the Scriptures which speak of the glory of Christ being seen by some of His at His public coming.

"The unbelieving remnant" were those who in the purpose of God were to be preserved for earthly blessing, being converted by the manifest appearing of Jesus.

Now, it is quite true that the Scripture does speak of two remnants in Israel: First, "The remnant shall return, even the remnant of Jacob unto the mighty God" (Isa. 10:21). This remnant that shall return is the spared of Israel who, after the judgments of the Lord, shall be the earthly people. Second, "At this present time also there is a remnant according to the election of grace" (Rom. 11:5). This remnant of Israel according to the election of grace, is that portion who, during this dispensation, believe in Christ; but in the Church they form no separate body; believing Jew and believing Gentile are one in Christ; and every Israelite led by the Holy Ghost to the blood of atonement now, is an integral part of the Church of the first-born. Thus, believing Jews who pass through the tribulation, and wait for the Lord's appearing, are in no sense separated from those who have gone before them.

It has been asked, If the saints come with Christ, must they not have been taken away before? and may not the interval be a long one, perhaps a whole age? The Scripture says that they are raised, and changed, and caught up to meet the Lord in the air, as He comes, and when He comes; and thus having met Him, they come with Him. If such a questioning as this were allowed to set aside plain testimonies, nothing in Scripture, however definite, would be certain.

It is in vain to imagine any "remnant according to the election of grace," except as part of the present Church.

THE HOPE OF CHRIST'S SECOND COMING

S. P. Tregelles

Chapter 15
Corroborative Passages:
'Wheat and Tares'

It is rarely found that the proofs of any leading truth of Scripture so depend one on another, that unless each proposition is demonstrated in its order, the whole fails: for habitually we find that the evidence of revealed verities is collateral; that is, there are many passages which prove a point if taken singly; and when looked at together they have a strong corroborative force.

In the parable of the wheat and the tares (Matt. 13:24–30; 36–43), Christ gives us some very simple instruction. The result of the sowing of the seed is that there is much wheat in the field: an enemy sows tares amongst them; and from that day until the harvest there is no point of time in which the field does not contain some of each. "Let both grow together until the harvest; and in the time of harvest I will say to the reapers, Gather ye together first the tares, and bind them in bundles to burn them; but gather the wheat into my barn" (verse 30). "As, therefore, the tares are gathered and burned in the fire, so shall it be in the end of this world [age]. The Son of man shall send forth His angels, and they shall gather out of His kingdom all things that offend, and them which do iniquity; and shall cast them into a furnace of fire: there shall be wailing and gnashing of teeth. Then shall the righteous shine forth as the sun in the kingdom of their Father" (verses 40–43).

Thus the removal of the Church, as set forth in the secret rapture theory, is impossible: for, from the moment of the first preaching of the gospel, until the angels are sent forth to sever the wicked from among the just, both classes are found mingled in Christendom. Had the secret rapture been the teaching of Christ, He could not have spoken of wheat as well as tares growing together until the harvest. For if the Church had been previously taken away, there would have been in the field tares, and tares only.

This contradicts also the notion of a body of Jewish believers being formed after the rapture of the Church; for unless the field were left, for awhile at least, free from wheat, and unless a new sowing altogether took place, this could not be. There is no such break or interval allowed in Scripture up to the time of the harvest, when "the righteous shine forth as the sun in the kingdom of their Father." (See Appendix D.)

S. P. Tregelles

Chapter 16
'Parousia' and 'Epiphaneia'

The Apostle Paul, himself the Apostle of the Gentiles, when writing to Gentile Churches or to individuals, holds forth the hope of the Lord's coming as that which is public, open, and manifest. Thus he describes believers as "looking for that blessed hope, and the appearing of the glory of our great God and Saviour Jesus Christ" (Titus 2:13). In writing to Timothy, he thus addresses the man of God: "I give thee charge in the sight of God, who quickeneth all things, and before Christ Jesus, who before Pontius Pilate witnessed a good confession, that thou keep this commandment without spot, unrebukeable, until the appearing of our Lord Jesus Christ" (1 Tim. 6:13, 14). In 2 Tim. 4:1, "the appearing and the kingdom" of our Lord are spoken of as truths of primary importance; and what they are to the believer is shown by verse 8; for there the Apostle says of our hope, "Henceforth there is laid up for me a crown of righteousness, which the Lord the righteous Judge, shall give me at that day; and not to me only, but unto all them also that love His appearing." This passage is enough to show that those who are looking to the coming of Christ in His manifest glory, have the true hope of His advent. Not a word or a hint is there on St. Paul's part that this

The Hope of Christ's Second Coming

coming shall be a secret thing: it is a manifestation in glory. One of the events of that point of time is the destruction of "the man of sin, whom the Lord shall consume with the Spirit of His mouth, and destroy with the brightness [or manifestation] of His coming" (2 Thess. 2:8). This is the same word as in the passages previously cited; in all these it belongs to our Lord's second coming; in its only other occurrence it relates to His first coming, when the Apostle speaks of God's "purpose and grace, which was given us in Christ Jesus before the world began, but is now made manifest by the appearing of our Saviour Jesus Christ" (2 Tim. 1:9,10). It is from the word rendered "appearing" (ἐπιφάνεια) that we derive our English term *epiphany*, applied to our Lord manifestly set forth as the incarnate Son of God.

The same Apostle speaks of the coming of Christ, for which the Church waits, as a revelation; thus the Corinthians are described as "waiting for the coming [margin, revelation] of our Lord Jesus Christ" (1 Cor. 1:7). The hope of the Thessalonians was "rest...when the Lord Jesus shall be revealed from heaven with His mighty angels, in flaming fire, taking vengeance on them that know not God, and that obey not the gospel of our Lord Jesus Christ; who shall be punished with everlasting destruction from the presence of the Lord, and from the glory of His power; when He shall come to be glorified in His saints, and to be admired in all them that believe (because our testimony among you was believed) in that day" (2 Thess. 1:7–11). If then the coming which the Church expects can be secret, then equally may all these particulars be secret also: but if secrecy is here intended as to the hopes of the Church, what words could be used which should unequivocally express open publicity?

Even if it were true that the writings of other apostles were "Jewish," surely those of the Apostle of the Gentiles could not be so restricted: and thus the point that our hope is the manifest appearing of our Lord (and no supposed secret coming) when proved by the teaching of St. Paul, ought to carry conviction even to those who introduce and teach such groundless distinctions.

It has indeed been said[13] that our hope is the coming of the Lord signified by another term (παρουσία), which is, they say, more strictly presence; and in contrast to this, they say, is His shining forth (ἐπιφάνεια), the word found in passages already cited, and rendered appearing; this, they say, is the Jewish hope. But, first, παρουσία, the word said to be connected with our hope, is habitually used for "coming" in ordinary expressions: thus, "the coming of Stephanas" (1 Cor. 16:17); "the coming of Titus" (2 Cor. 7:6, see, too, verse 7); "my coming to you again." (Phil. 1:26).

Second. This word, which is said to imply a hope for the Church of a secret coming, is that which is used in Matthew 24 (the very chapter which some would represent to be Jewish), in speaking of our Lord's public and glorious appearing. In verse 3, the disciples ask, "What shall be the sign of thy coming?" Our Lord, in His reply,

---

[13] So little had I heard of this argument on the words ἐπιφάνεια and παρουσία for many years (ever since 1839, when it seemed to be abandoned for other theories), that I should have scarcely thought it needful to notice it, had I not found that it was again revived. I well remember how some used to press it, and how unspiritual they thought the endeavor to show how these words are really used in the New Testament. It is one of the cases in which the attempt has been made to misrepresent the facts of Scripture, and in which the uninstructed and unwary have been misled.

The Hope of Christ's Second Coming

says, "As the lightning cometh out of the east, and shineth even unto the west, so shall also the coming of the Son of Man be" (verse 27). "Then shall all the tribes of the earth mourn, and they shall see the Son of man coming in the clouds of heaven with power and great glory" (verse 30). This, then, is that coming which shall be as the lightning in open visibility. "As the days of Noe were, so shall also the coming of the Son of man be. For as in the days that were before the flood, they were eating and drinking, marrying and giving in marriage, until the day that Noe entered into the ark, and knew not until the flood came, and took them all away; so shall also the coming of the Son of man be" (verses 37–39). Is this a secret coming known only to the Church, and not affecting others?

Third. The word ἐπιφάνεια, which, on the supposition now under consideration, has to do with the visible appearing of our Lord at some period subsequent to the rapture of the Church, is that which, in Titus 2:13, 1 Tim. 6:14, and 2 Tim. 4:8, is given as the hope of that very Church, whose existence on earth at the time is denied by such theories. This word is not used, except in 2 Thess. 2:8, in connection with others besides the Church.

When one event is spoken of in various aspects, different words may be rightly used; and thus παρουσία is the most general term for that one coming of our Lord, which is the object of the Church's hope. Those who have mystified the minds of the uninstructed by incorrect teaching as to the use of the words of Scripture, incur a solemn responsibility; they obtain an advantage as teachers, based wholly on rash assertions; the best that can be supposed of such is that they "understand neither what they say, nor whereof they affirm." But they are responsible for misleading others by their assertions, for the sin of ignorance is still sin. (See Appendix E.)

The Hope of Christ's Second Coming

S. P. Tregelles

Chapter 17
Watch!

But are not believers called on to watch? Is not the exhortation, "Watch, therefore, for ye know not what hour your Lord doth come?" Does not this injunction apply to us? and how can we thus watch if there are any previous events predicted? Does not this passage show that the momentary expectation that our Lord may come is that which we should rightly cherish? This exhortation is given us in Matt. 24:42, the very chapter which some say is "Jewish," and its reference is to that coming spoken of in the context, which is one of public manifestation, and one which is introduced by signs. But it has already been stated that the rejection of the force and bearing of Scriptures, because they are said to be "Jewish," is a groundless assumption; and thus, if any choose to quote a few words from such portions in defense of a supposed secret advent, no objection is to be made on that ground; but the connection has to be shown between the words quoted and the true doctrine of the Lord's coming, with which He has Himself associated them.

The coming spoken of is one as manifest as the lightning, as definite as the judgment of the flood. Its date is not revealed, so that it cannot be measured by years or

THE HOPE OF CHRIST'S SECOND COMING

centuries; but there are indications which will speak definitely to those who are truly watching. To this purpose the parable of the fig-tree was spoken, of which the application is, "So likewise ye, when ye shall see all these things, know that it is nigh, even at the doors" (verse 33).[14] It is to persons thus instructed that the charge is given to watch: they are not told to watch irrespective of signals, but to be ready to note them as they appear. "What, then (it is said), are we to wait for signs, and not for the Lord Himself?" But what does such a question mean? If the Lord has told us so to wait, it is thus that we should watch. To despise the sign is to despise the Word of the Lord who has promised it; it is to refuse submission to His authority. If an absent master has told his servants to wait for his return, which shall be intimated by a letter that he will send, are they obeyers of his word if they say that they expect him before the arrival of his promised letter, or if, when the letter arrives, they neglect it, and say that it is not for them? Those who expect it not, although told, might well do this.

"Let your loins be girded about, and your lights burning; and ye yourselves like unto men that wait for their lord, when he will return from the wedding; that when he cometh and knocketh, they may open to him immediately. Blessed are those servants whom the lord when he cometh shall find watching: verily I say unto you, that he shall gird himself, and make them to sit down to meat, and will come forth, and serve them....Be ye therefore ready also; for the Son of Man cometh at an

---

[14] "The budding of the fig-tree" is especially considered in my *Remarks on the Prophetic Visions of the Book of Daniel* (pp. 1–6. Fifth edition, 1864. To avoid mere repetition, I refer to what has there been said.

hour when ye think not" (Luke 12:35–37,40). Thus the hope of His coming does not exclude that His knock shall be first heard; nay, this signal is presupposed. Let it also be noted that the same passages which speak of our being called to watch, as not knowing the day or the hour, are those in which special prominence is given to the manifest advent of the Lord, so that these definitely exclude any thought of a supposed secret coming being that for which we are called to wait.

But, it is said, is not the supposition that events must precede the coming of the Lord that which is meant by the servant saying, "My lord delayeth his coming?" Is not the admission of such a thought sinful? In Matthew 24 and Luke 12 the servant is spoken of who says this; but his sin is not the knowledge that he has of intervening events, but the mode in which he acts, though having such supposed intelligence. "But and if that evil servant shall say in his heart, My lord delayeth his coming; and shall begin to smite his fellow servants, and to eat and drink with the drunken; the lord of that servant shall come in a day when he looketh not for him, and in an hour that he is not aware of; and shall cut him asunder, and appoint him his portion with the hypocrites." His sin is the use which he makes of his partial knowledge, instead of his employing it to lead him the more definitely to watch for the promised indication of his master's coming. He who looks for promised events as indications of the Lord's advent, will not rest for a moment in the events themselves: their value is, that they lead on the thoughts and affections to Him for whom the Church is called to watch and wait, and who has Himself promised these signs to His expecting people. (See Appendix F.)

The Hope of Christ's Second Coming

To watch unscripturally is really not to watch at all; but to substitute something of emotion and sentiment for "the patient waiting for Christ."

S. P. Tregelles

Chapter 18
Are Signs Jewish?

"But are not signs Jewish? Are they not intended only for Israel? and, if so, would not attention to them distract us from our true hope?" A pointed question may convey a true or false thought in argumentation; it may remind of some true and fully admitted principle, or it may suggest the adoption of some fallacy as though it were a revealed truth.

Now, if signs were "Jewish," indicating the glorious appearing of the Messiah, since there is but one Christ, and His coming in glory is the promise to His Church, they would be of equal significance to us, for they would instruct us as much as they would Jews. But on what ground are "signs" said to be "Jewish"? Our Lord's words are: "A wicked and adulterous generation seeketh after a sign; and there shall no sign be given unto it but the sign of the prophet Jonas" (Matt. 16:4). "Why doth this generation seek after a sign? verily I say unto you, There shall no sign be given unto this generation" (Mark 8:12). To the generation of Israel, rejecting the resurrection of Jesus ("the sign of the prophet Jonas"), no sign shall be given. This unbelieving generation, from which Peter exhorted his hearers to save themselves (Acts 2:40), marked by the same moral characteristics, will not pass away until the things spoken of in Matthew 24 shall be accomplished in the manifestation of the glory of the Lord: and thus signs cannot be for them. "This generation" cannot mean the men then alive merely, for if so Israel would long ago have owned Jesus of Nazareth. "As the lightning that lighteneth out of the one part under heaven shineth unto the other part under heaven, so shall also the Son of Man be in His day; but first must He suffer many things, and be rejected of this generation" (Luke 17:24,25). Unconverted Jews have said from this passage that, if Jesus had been a true prophet, the next generation of Israel would have believed on Him, for it was by that generation He was to be rejected. The argument is legitimate; the only fallacy is that of imagining that "generation" means the men then living. The future generation of Israel shall believe.

No sign shall be given to unconverted Israel "this generation" rejecting the Son of Man: and any portion of Israel converted is essentially a portion of the Church, even as the Pentecostal saints were all Jews.

But the Lord has promised signs ("There shall be signs in the sun, and in the moon, and in the stars," Luke 21:25), and these signs can only be for His believing people. They are closely connected with our watchfulness. We wait for the budding of the fig-tree. "When these things begin to come to pass, then look up and lift up your heads, for your redemption draweth nigh" (Luke 21:28).

S. P. Tregelles

Chapter 19
Secret Rapture — Scriptures Contradictory

Those who deny the Pentateuch to be a revelation given through Moses, have often pointed out the periods in the history of Israel in which the most plain commands of the law were set aside, either by neglect, or by direct and positive contravention.

Thus when, in the days of the Judges, the people so often practiced idolatry, how is it possible (it has been said) that they could have a law which so positively forbids all worship save that of the true God, and any religious honor to be paid to any image or picture? Is it not evident that the Mosaic law must have been a subsequent invention? If in the days of Jeroboam, the son of Nebat, the people had possessed the law, how could that king have ventured to set it aside in all essentials? May we not (they say) conclude that the law which forbids all image worship, which limits the priesthood to a particular family, which prohibits sacrifice except in the place that God chose, and which defines so precisely at what period in the year the stated feasts should be observed, was then unknown? and, if unknown, could it then exist?

The Hope of Christ's Second Coming

Skeptical questionings of this kind have a certain weight; but they at once fall to the ground when confronted with even the smallest quantity of fact; and if they had really any conclusive force, we must know that in the same way it might be said that the Christian Church cannot in general have possessed the New Testament. And if it be said that in many lands even now the Scripture is withheld from the people, so that no counter-argument can be drawn from its being practically set aside, yet in this country there is no such restriction; and thus any manner in which it is ignored amongst us, illustrates the way in which the law was neglected often by Israel of old; or, as in the days of our Lord, made of no effect through the tradition which had virtually supplanted it.

Now, it is very remarkable that those who have the Scripture, and who read it with some measure of attention, can have adopted or received a system which contradicts some of the simplest statements of our Lord and His inspired apostles; thus we can feel no surprise that there was a similar setting aside of the early portion of revelation: and as we find that this system is defended, so we may well imagine that there were some who could defend the proceedings and practices of the days of Jeroboam, "who made Israel to sin."

Our Lord has promised that He will return in the clouds of heaven with power and great glory, and that then He will send forth His angels to gather His elect. The secret advent doctrine teaches that He will come privately, and that then He will raise His sleeping saints and change the living, taking them up to Himself a good while before His manifestation.

The Scripture warns the saints of perilous times, and of evils in the latter day before the coming of Christ. The secret advent theory maintains that no such events can be known as would interpose an interval between the present moment and the coming of the Lord.

The Scripture speaks only of Christ's second coming, until which He remains at the right hand of God the Father. The secret advent is a notion entirely opposed to this; for it represents our Lord first coming in a private manner to take the Church to meet Him, and then at a future period (according to some, a long interval) coming in glory; and this some call His third coming.

The Scripture teaches the Church to wait for the manifestation of Christ. The secret theory bids us to expect a coming before any such manifestation.

Our Lord says that the wheat and tares shall be together in the field until the harvest. The doctrine of the secret rapture affirms that at some time considerably before the harvest, all the wheat shall have been removed, leaving only tares.

Our Lord bids us look for certain signs, and use them in our watching. The advocates of the secret advent contradict this, saying that signs are not for us.

The Scripture tells us that the first resurrection of the saints will be when the Lord has come forth as the conqueror, and that those will share in this resurrection who have suffered under the final Antichrist. The teachers of the secret doctrine say that the resurrection of the present Church will take place long before the first resurrection,[15] and before the manifestation of the Antichrist.

---

[15] In 1839, I heard it maintained with such approbation that objectors were hardly allowed a hearing, that if strictly correct language were used, the first resurrection of Revelation 20 would be called "the SECOND-first resurrection;" for it was said that "the FIRST-first resurrection" would have taken place privately a good while before. Is it not a sitting in judgment

The Hope of Christ's Second Coming

Is it not surprising that men with their Bibles in their hands, can be led to adopt a theory of doctrine which not only adds to Scripture, but contradicts it at all points? This is just the simple and natural consequence of the acceptance of the one leading addition to Scripture, that there shall be a secret coming of the Lord, and a secret rapture of His Church.

When Christ distinctly states a truth, it might have been expected that at least those who profess to be His believing people would receive His words as conclusive; and thus it might have been thought that those only who avowedly reject His authority would deny the force of what He said. Now our Lord has expressly taught us that His coming shall not be secret: He has told us this, not only by saying that it will be manifest, but also by warning against any supposition of such a secret coming as suits some of the "Jewish" notions. After speaking of the unequalled tribulation, He says, "Then if any man shall say unto you, lo, here is Christ, or there, believe it not. For there shall arise false Christs and false prophets, and shall show great signs and wonders; insomuch that, if it were possible, they shall deceive the very elect. Behold, I have told you before. Wherefore, if they shall say unto you, Behold, He is in the desert, go not forth; behold, He is in the secret chambers, believe it not. For as the lightning cometh out of the east, and shineth even unto the west, so shall also the coming of the Son of Man be" (Matt. 24:23–27). No man with these words in his Bible, ought to accept the doctrine of any secret coming without feeling

---

on Holy Scripture when endeavors are thus made to correct and to improve the words used by the Spirit of God? No one would do this unless he felt in his conscience the force of the words of inspiration, and struggled to set them aside.

that he is casting off, in so doing, the authority of the Lord; for this is done, virtually, when the warning of Christ is treated as if He had taught the very reverse, and as if He had charged us to believe and expect what, in reality, He says shall never be, and against the supposition of which He warns us.

The Hope of Christ's Second Coming

S. P. Tregelles

Chapter 20
The Day of the Lord:
Canticles and Apocalypse

When a point has been established by full proof from Holy Scripture, it is often impossible, and in general needless, to meet each objection or difficulty which may be raised. It is often impossible, because all the modes in which different objectors will find difficulties may be unknown to those who rest on the simple warrants of the Word of God. It is commonly needless, because when we have to do with those who are subject to the authority of God in His Word, full Scripture proof of a point is enough; and also it is felt that the varying grounds taken by objectors, and their contradictions of Scripture, show that they are striving (even though at times unconsciously) against truths which cannot be overthrown.

Thus, if we have to establish the Deity of Christ, we bring forward the direct proofs, the distinct statements that He is God over all, blessed for ever, and that He is the Creator, Sustainer, and essentially the Lord of all. We do not think it needful to inquire into every cavil of every objector, and to discuss these one by one, before we regard the point as proved. We do not pretend to meet what may be called the difficulties of the case; indeed, we do wisely not to imagine that we can overcome the prejudice which is proof against the distinct words of inspired prophets and apostles. We have, as well as we are enabled, to state the revealed truth; and then its application can be made with efficacious power by the secret working of the Holy Ghost.

Although reference has been made to particular objections, to discuss them in detail has not been attempted. The reasons just stated will suffice for this: answers have been given to some of the ways in which the Scriptures cited have been set aside; but beyond this it is impossible to go without an extensive inquiry into the various modes in which advocates of the secret coming and secret rapture seek to make the theory plausible. It would be as much to the purpose to discuss all that has been written against the truth that "we are justified freely by the grace of God, for the sake of Christ's merits, through faith," before firmly and definitely setting forth the Gospel. All the grounds of objection to the hope of Christ's people being His glorious appearing, to which I refer, are such as really have been relied on. I do not discuss mere surmises; I notice a few points for the help (as I trust) of some; but I do not charge any one with holding anything which he rejects: different maintainers of the secret rapture have taken different grounds.

A supposed distinction has been made between the coming of Christ and the day of the Lord, as if the one could be a secret hope before the other which is manifest; but in 1 Cor. 1:8, "the day of our Lord" is the hope of the Church: so, too, in 2 Cor. 1:14, is "the day of the Lord Jesus;" in Phil. 1:6,10 believers are directed on to "the day of Jesus Christ;" in 1 Thess. 5:2, Christians are spoken of as knowing that the day of the Lord cometh like "a thief in the night," but (verses 4,5) it will not come like a thief on those who are children of light; but still it is the day that they expect. In 2 Thess. 2:1,2, "the coming of our Lord Jesus Christ," and "the day of the Lord" (true reading) are used as co-ordinate terms. And well may this be done; for at the coming of the Lord Jesus the day begins: the only contrast that could be drawn is, that the coming is one point of time, while the day is a continuous period: to those who are in the darkness of night, however, it is the same thing to expect the dawn of the sunlight and the beginning of the day: and he who tried to distinguish these things as to time, would fail in finding intelligible language in which to express himself. In 2 Peter 3:12, believers are spoken of as "looking for and hasting unto the coming of the day of God;" this is the same "day of the Lord" which verse 10 speaks of as the fulfillment of "the promise of His [Christ's] coming" (verse 4), about which the scoffer asks, as if it were a hope that had failed. The passages which speak of the day as our hope contradict all theory of secrecy. Could the Sun of Righteousness arise without the day beginning? Had a distinction been made the dawn would precede the sun-rising.

Some, indeed, ask, "Have you not overlooked how plainly the secret rapture of the Church is set forth in the Canticles?" But is it intended that we should interpret the New Testament by the Canticles? Should we not rather let the full light of the Christian Revelation shine on the ancient Scriptures? Of one thing we may be certain, that nothing in the Canticles can contradict our Lord's words, and His promise that His elect shall be gathered unto Him by His angels at His manifest coming with power and great glory. Whatever may be the import of passages in the Canticles which speak of secrecy ("the secret[16] places of the

---

[16] I could hardly give the supposed detail how "the clefts of the rock" became "the secret places of the stairs," without

stairs," etc.), or of the withdrawal of the bride from any particular scene ("Come with me from Lebanon," etc.), we ought to be so established in New Testament truth as not to imagine that these can set forth a secret rapture, unless such a rapture had been definitely taught in the Word instead of its being contradicted.

To learn the distinct hope of the Lord's coming is a far simpler thing than it is to interpret the Canticles. Many may know definitely the promises of our Lord, who can but ponder as to that book, valuing it not according to their intelligence of its contents, but because they see Christ there.[17]

Others ask whether it is not evident that the Church is seen in the Book of Revelation in heavenly glory, long

---

going beyond that gravity and reverence for Holy Scripture that should be maintained.

[17] That this book has a holy character is what few, I trust, who read these pages, will doubt: that it must set forth Christ is what reverential readers of Holy Scripture will of course admit. The theories of Ewald and others must be abhorrent to every Christian mind; and although Ginsburg seeks to give a new turn to such theories, yet it is vain to make the subject of the book of Canticles a shepherdess, who contemns and finally rejects the addresses of King Solomon. The grounds on which Ginsburg excludes Christ, and adopts, with less irreverence of expression, notions borrowed from Ewald, etc., are of the weakest kind. Even unconverted Jews, such as Aben Ezra, could teach him better. It would be marvelous that he should find followers, except that any notion which unsettles definite thoughts as to Holy Scripture, or which would exclude Christ, is sure to be admired by some. Dean Alford has well said that he who does not find Christ everywhere in Holy Scripture, will not be able to find Him anywhere. "This is a great mystery, but I speak concerning Christ and the Church."

before the visible coming of our Lord. (See Appendix G.) Now, our hopes may be known very clearly, even though we have but little ability to interpret the Apocalypse; nay, it is rather by apprehending our hopes that we shall begin to use that closing book of Scripture aright.

The teachers of the "secret" doctrine act in very contradictory ways with regard to the Apocalypse. Some of them say that it is not for our instruction, for it is given from Christ to show "His servants things which must shortly come to pass" (See concluding paragraphs of Chapter 11); others say that the epistles to the seven churches are our portion ("the things which are"); but that when a door is opened in heaven (Chapter 4) the Church is caught up. Others maintain that the whole book is future; that the seven churches even are bodies which shall be formed (and which shall be thus taught), after the secret removal of the present Church. Now, without discussing these contradictory theories, let it be again noted that the coming of the Lord is set forth in the opening of the book: "Behold, He cometh with clouds, and every eye shall see him;" and to this coming, the Apostle responds, "Even so, Amen." No supposition that the Church is found in resurrection glory prior to such a coming can be admitted as capable of reconciliation with this opening expectation. Nor can any symbol be rightly interpreted as setting forth the Church as actually in resurrection glory at a point of time previous to the first resurrection of Chapter 20, and that is after the last anti-Christian persecution, in which the faithful are beheaded because of the testimony of Jesus.[18]

---

[18] Much has been made, in connection with the supposed secret rapture of the Church, of the description of the throne, etc., in [Revelation] Chapters 4 and 5, and of the living creatures and elders. Chapters 5, 9, 10, is a passage which

THE HOPE OF CHRIST'S SECOND COMING

If the manifest coming of our Lord in glory be not our hope, it would be indeed strange that the apostles

---

has been thought to have an especial bearing on this subject. The true reading of the verses is, "And they sing a new song, saying, Thou art worthy to take the book, and to open the seals thereof; for thou wast slain, and redeemedst us to God by thy blood out of every tribe, and tongue, and people, and nation; (10) and thou madest them to our God a kingdom and priests, and they reign on the earth." That verse 10 should be read in the third person αὐτοὺς, and βασιλεύουσιν, (or, -σουσιν), instead of ἡμᾶς and βασιλεύσομεν, is not at all a matter of doubt; whether the verb should be in the future or in the present is less certain. But in verse 9, ἡμᾶς, "us," should certainly be read. There was an opinion, many years ago, that it rested on but slight authority. This arose through an error in a reprint of Griesbach's text; so that he was supposed to have excluded it. On this misprint interpretations were based. Now of all collated manuscripts, the *Codex Alexandrinus* alone omits ἡμᾶς (and this is thought to have some support from the Ethiopic version); and one manuscript has ἡμῶν instead. The consent of the ancient versions has much weight in a case of this kind. It is surprising that some later editors have omitted it only on the authority mentioned. Its absence appears to have some supposed bearing on the present question. A maintainer of the secret rapture, in publishing a text of the Revelation, gave a few readings professedly from the *Codex Sinaiticus*, in which he prints, by some strange hallucination, τῷ θ.ἡμῶν as the reading of that manuscript. This was at first copied by Dean Alford in his Greek Testament, and in Mr. C. E. Stuart's very useful little work, *Textual Criticism*; so that the error has become widely spread. But *Codex Sinaiticus* reads τω θεω ἡμας, exactly like the common text. I have seen the passage in the manuscript itself, and any one can verify it in the two editions of Tischendorf. How the omission of ἡμᾶς could be made to support the secret rapture doctrine I do not at all know.

should have so habitually taught such a coming, and have said so much about it in their epistles.

If the secret advent and secret removal of the Church be true, how can the advocates of this theory show that the secret event did not take place long ago? How do they know but that they themselves are living in the supposed interval between the secret coming of Christ and His coming in glory? And thus, how can they be sure that they are part of the Church at all? In fact, if the secret rapture theory were true, they might be devoid of all knowledge of what way of salvation (amongst the confused theories) is now available; for the preaching of the Gospel may have ended with the rapture and resurrection of the Church; and, if this is a private occurrence, it may be long past, without any one being aware of it.

THE HOPE OF CHRIST'S SECOND COMING

S. P. Tregelles

Chapter 21
'Times and Seasons'

"But do you not remember," it is said, "that God holds the times and seasons in His own power? Does not this shew that He may arrange events as He willeth—that He may re-dispose their order? And is not the definite formation of expectations, as if God must bring events to pass in one way and not in another, a limiting of the Holy One of Israel?" God has all things in His power; but when once He has spoken, He will fulfill; and thus, without irreverence, we may say that such event will occur, and such will not. When once God has promised, He is concluded by His own words: He cannot deny Himself. Thus we may, with all confidence, say, that if God has revealed that a portion of His Church shall be found in unbroken continuity on the earth up to the harvest, when the wicked shall be severed from the midst of them, then so it will be. If He has said that Antichrist's appearance and power shall precede the coming of Christ, then this must be the order of events. If He tells us that it is after, and not before, the time of special tribulation that Christ shall come, then we must not discredit God by the imagination that it may be previous. If the Lord Jesus has told us that His shall not be a secret coming, then we must take heed and not accept the teaching that bids us expect a secret advent. If He tells us to watch for His appointed signs, then we must not imagine that this can be inconsistent with the hope of seeing the Lord, or that it can have any evil effect morally; nay, we must be sure that such an expectation, held in the Spirit, is that which will produce the right effect of watchfulness and waiting in every one who rests on the word of Christ, because it is His.

However much God may do in grace and mercy beyond what He has promised, of this we may be sure, that whatever He has promised shall be fulfilled; and that every revealed circumstance in connection with the time or order shall have a perfect accomplishment. In unrevealed things, it behooves us to avoid speculation; but where the Scripture speaks, it is for us, whether we understand or not, to listen and to receive.

In any inquiry what God can do, or will do, there are two principles which must be borne in mind: Firstly, God is "the faithful God;" "God that cannot lie." This is part of His own essential character; and we know, too, that as to His revelation in Christ, "all the promises of God in Him are yea, and in Him Amen, to the glory of God by us" (2 Cor. 1:20). Secondly, besides this (or rather consequent on this), "the Scripture must be fulfilled." What can prove this more fully than our Lord's prayer and agony in the garden, and His betrayal? "O my Father, if it be possible, let this cup pass from me: nevertheless not as I will, but as thou wilt" (Matt. 26:39). "O my Father, if this cup may not pass from me, except I drink it, thy will be done" (verse 42). "Thinkest thou that I cannot now pray to my Father, and He shall presently give me more than twelve legions of angels? But how then shall the Scriptures be fulfilled, that thus it must be?" (verses 53, 54). "But all this was done that the Scriptures of the prophets might be fulfilled" (verse 56).

If there are points which are not certainly or definitely stated in Scripture, some conclusion may, perhaps, be formed from analogy or probable inference; but when the Scripture tells the events and their order, then what is called "free enquiry" has no place whatever. Those who sit in judgment on Scripture, and question or deny what it conclusively says, are not fitting persons to be listened to as teachers in the Church of Christ, whatever be their claims as to wisdom or holiness.

The question of the apostles to the Lord in Acts 1:6 is, "Lord, wilt thou at this time restore again the kingdom to Israel?" To this He replies, "It is not for you to know the times or the seasons, which the Father hath put in His own power." He then tells them what their service should be as witnesses for Him—in fact, referring them back to His own previous instruction in Matt. 24:6,14: "The end is not yet." "And this gospel of the kingdom shall be preached in all the world for a witness unto all nations; and then shall the end come." They are thus reminded that the restoration of the kingdom to Israel could not be in the ordering of God until the events of that chapter were brought to pass; it was thus that He had put these times and seasons in His own power. We cannot measure these events by a century or by a thousand years, but we may know their order as revealed and recorded in Holy Scripture.

When the Apostle says, "I would not, brethren, that ye should be ignorant of this mystery...that blindness in part is happened to Israel, UNTIL the fulness of the Gentiles be come in" (Rom. 11:25), the following words, "And so all Israel shall be saved," prove that the blindness shall be altogether taken away. But when shall this be?

The Hope of Christ's Second Coming

When the fullness of the Gentiles is gathered. How could the Scripture speak of a "blindness in part until" that time, if Israel's greatest blindness, in the depth of anti-Christian evil, is not till after the removal of the Church? But the order of these events has been revealed for our instruction. It is when He cometh with clouds, when every eye shall see Him, that Israel shall look on Him whom they pierced—when the Spirit of Grace and of Supplications shall be poured upon them. Until that day the fullness of the Gentiles will not have come in. The resurrection of the Church and the removal of the blindness are at the same time.

S. P. Tregelles

Chapter 22
Sentiment and Emotion:
The Truth of God

There is sternness in the truth of God, which might almost seem like harsh severity, when it is regarded by those whose thoughts on the subject of revelation have been formed in a great measure from sentiment and emotion. An imaginative feeling may exist; and this may be so cherished that even the Scripture is only used for sentimental purposes; and thus the force of definite truth is by no means felt, because the mind has sunk into a kind of spiritual reverie: indeed, there is a disposition to avoid definite truth, from a contrast that has been formed between it and that which is supposed to be spiritual. Thus when the details of revealed promises and purposes are stated from the Word of God, there is a feeling that there is but little, if anything, in them that is really edifying, or that can afford nourishment for spiritual life. And thus dreamy indefinite thoughts of God's love are cherished, and such a view is taken of the person and work of Christ, and of His coming glory, as may stir up spiritual emotions, or what are supposed to be such. But it must never be forgotten that holiness is not the only thing taught us respecting the Holy Ghost: He is the Spirit of Truth as

The Hope of Christ's Second Coming

well as the Holy Spirit of God; and the two things should be combined, and not set in contrast. We are not to accredit any supposed holiness irrespective of truth; we are not to regard truth as rightly held unless it be connected with holiness: and as truth is found in the revelation given in Holy Scripture, this must be our standard by which we must judge whatever professes to be either holiness, such as God would approve, or truth, that His people should accept.

Emotional religion has always a tendency to make feeling the standard of what should be received as truth, and what rejected. A certain kind of high wrought feeling (approaching to mysticism, or amounting to it) is that which is allowed to rule the judgment as to whatever God has revealed; and some times these indefinite claims to spirituality are accepted by others, so that the doctrines of such teachers are supposed to be worthy of all acceptance, not because they are found in Holy Scripture, but because they are said to be true by such holy and devoted men. But if we would judge according to God, we must test all claims to holiness and devotedness by means of truth, and not merely do the reverse. Asceticism is not Christian holiness; the zeal of Francis Xavier is not Christian devotedness.

It is very manifest that the doctrine of a secret coming of Christ, and a secret removal of the Church to be with Him, is peculiarly suited to those who cherish the religion of sentiment.[19] What more cheering (they say)

---

[19] It is as impossible to discuss a question scripturally with those who are guided by emotion and sentiment, as it was for Greatheart, in the second part of *Pilgrim's Progress*, to arouse Heedless and Too—bold when sleeping on the Enchanted Ground.

than the thought that the Lord may take His people to Himself at any moment? What more animating than the belief that this may take place this very day? And when any one brings them to Scripture, and tries to point out the revealed hope of the Lord's coming, it seems as if there were nothing but coldness in the teaching, and as if the Lord were put far off from them. They ask sometimes if such chilling doctrines can be consistent with love to the Lord, and whether love to His person does not exclude the thought of a revealed interval, and of events that will take place first. It is thus that truth is judged by sentiment and emotion, instead of true emotions, which are according to God, being formed by truth in all its definite severity. Whatever makes the feelings sit in judgment on Scripture, and whatever thus leads to the avoidance of the force of that Scripture teaching which is not in accordance with such feelings, must, however apparently sanctified and spiritual, be of nature, and not of God. Are we to seek to be guided by other hopes than those which animated the Apostolic Church? They knew that days of darkness would set in before Christ's coming; they were instructed respecting the many Antichrists and the final Antichrist, but so far from their hope of the coming of the Lord and of resurrection being thus set aside, they were able to look onward through the darkness to the brightness of the morning.

It may freely be owned that those who think it right to expect the Lord at any moment, and who sternly condemn others who maintain that His appointed signals shall take place first, have often in their hearts much real love to Him; and love towards His person is never to be regarded lightly. But let such remember the prayer of the Apostle, "That your love may abound yet more and more in knowledge and in all judgment" (Phil. 1:9): it is not only of importance that love should be rightly directed as to its object, but also that there should be in the soul real spiritual intelligence. If a wife has the promise of her husband's return from a distant country, and she has his written directions for the rule of the house during his absence, and part of these directions includes a statement how his return shall be expected, that a letter will first arrive to say by what ship he will come—there would be no want of love (and that, too, intelligent love) on her part, if she sought to be occupied day by day as he directed, and if she showed that she believed his word that the promised letter should come, and that then he would himself arrive by the appointed vessel. She would be waiting according to his word and will; and no one could reproach her for want of love to her lord from not being on the tip-toe of momentary expectation. But if the wife were to say that the part of her husband's directions respecting the promised letter related to the servants of the house, and not to her, and if she were to be constantly on the shore, expecting her husband's landing in a way that he had not promised, and if she refused to be brought to attend simply to what her husband had said she would, while professing to do this out of love to him, show that she was a visionary, and not one whose love was guided by the simple intelligence of her husband's mind as distinctly expressed: feeling would have led away from true obedience.

  There are, indeed, those who say that love can allow of nothing as between their souls and the coming of the Lord; they avoid any real scriptural inquiry on the subject; and when events prophesied by our Lord are pointed out, they say that their views are directed upward, that there they find their strength, in contrast to "men's hearts failing them for fear, and for looking after those things which are coming on the earth" (Luke 21:26). And thus they avoid the force of even our Lord's words, through a supposed spirituality. Men's hearts may be dismayed, but this will not apply to believers, who would see in that which caused dismay to others the bright prospect of deliverance to themselves, for the coming of the Lord would be at hand.

The dreamy ethereality, which assumes the name and the garb of spirituality, avoids the apprehension of facts; they appear too unrefined, and there is too little in them for the exercise of mere sentimental feeling. But is it not by facts, and facts too occurring on this earth, that God works? The incarnation of the Son of God, the reality of His meritorious obedience, of His vicarious sufferings, the atonement of the Cross—all, indeed, on which we depend for salvation—have to do with facts which have taken place on this earth. Though Christ is at the right hand of God, yet here He wrought out those facts in all their literal truth, on which the forgiveness of sins, and the acceptance of our persons, depend. Why, then, avoid the contemplation of those facts which are yet before us, in all their definiteness of detail?

Sentimental religion often approaches very nearly to mere ideality: the ideal Christ takes in part the place of the Christ of revelation, and although it cannot be denied by any one professing to be a Christian that the literal blood of atonement was shed here on the literal Cross, yet so far from seeing that the redemption price was paid to the full when Christ said, "It is finished," and died, they speak of the real atonement having not been made until Jesus, risen from the dead, presented His own blood on the mercy seat above. Thus (with various modifications) they speak and write about salvation and justification in "the risen Jesus," not seeing that His work in connection with sin was completed for ever on the Cross.[20]

But real love is no mere ideality: it is an active thing. God's love was shown in providing the salvation wrought out by His blessed Son; and if we have true Christian love in our hearts it will be found an active principle also, both towards God and towards the brethren for His sake. Yet how often have we seen sentimental love fail altogether: it has been much set forth in word, but the moment that it has been tested, its merely emotional character has been proved. The false principle of mysticism as to the love of God is, that He loves His own image which His grace and Spirit work in us: this is much the same as saying that He loves us so far as He sees us worthy of His love, or as He

---

[20] Romans 4:25 plainly teaches that our Lord "was delivered in consequence of our offences, and raised again in consequence of our justification." The preposition in each case is the same, so that just as His death resulted from His bearing our sins, so did His resurrection result from the accomplishment of that propitiation whereby we receive pardon and peace. Some speak of our sins "being buried in the grave of Jesus;" but how could they get there? The Cross was the last place where He had to do with sin: the shedding of His blood, the laying down of His life, was the payment of the full redemption price. He himself bore our sins up to the tree; but on the completion of His sacrifice, all that had to do with sin was ended; and He was laid in the grave, not as then the sinbearer, but as the Holy One who had borne the full penalty. Of this the resurrection was the full proof. If the weight of sin rested on Him when buried, how could it have been removed? It is true that our sin had laid Him in the grave, because He had died to put it away; but it was no longer on Him when He was there. On Rom. 4:25, see, as to this point, Bishop Horsley's sermon *Nine Sermons on our Lord's Resurrection*, etc., p. 249. 1822.

sees some congruity in us. If the love of God be so regarded, the love to the brethren may well be of the same character: love not for the Father's sake, not for Christ's sake, but for the sake of some inwrought fitness in the object. Those who make sentimentally the secret rapture the center of all their thoughts, have habitually shown how utterly their love fails towards any Christians who object to this theory. They often speak of them as if such were devoid of love to Christ, and they treat them as if that were the case. It might seem as if they had made that one point (in which they are led by feeling, not by Scripture) the very test of Christian profession. They ask, indeed, with earnestness of manner, how those who deny the secret advent can "love His appearing,"[21] and they refer to the passage (Heb. 9:28) "Unto them that look for Him shall He appear the second time, without sin, unto salvation," as if it included only those who hold a peculiar expectation. To these it is that they extend their mystical love, which has so much taken the place of what is truly Christian.

But "they that look for Him" does not mean a part of the Church, but the whole; not those who expect in a particular manner, but those who know that as He died, rose, and ascended, so surely He will come again, as has been promised. It does not depend on the intelligence of

---

[21] If it were desirable to answer arguments in the same way as that in which they are put, it might be asked whether those who expect a secret coming of Christ are those "that love His appearing"? For this is of necessity a manifest thing. But at least let not the advocates of a secret coming speak of those who expect the appearing of Christ, as if they failed in that love to Him which should lead them to wait for Him. They love His appearing, and they do not substitute something else in the place of "that blessed hope."

The Hope of Christ's Second Coming

believers, or the reverse. The fact has been embodied in the common expressions of Christian belief: "He shall come again with glory to judge both the quick and the dead: whose kingdom shall have no end" (the Nicene Creed); "Thou sittest on the right hand of God, in the glory of the Father. We believe that thou shalt come to be our Judge" (*Te Deum*). Such, even in the darkest ages, has been the profession of the nominal Church; such has been ever the solemn acknowledgment of true believers. If they inquired but little about the circumstances of that coming, or the connected events, who would dare, even in thought, to exclude them from the number of those who love the appearing of the Lord Jesus Christ? Who would say that they are not of "those that look for Him?" (See Appendix H.)

Such sentimental feeling, when allowed full outflowing in connection with the doctrine of the secret advent, works this, amongst other evils—the narrowing, both in practice and in principle, of that Christian love which should be directed towards all who are in Christ, and which should include all living believers, and all who from the beginning have obtained a good report through faith.

It is almost impossible to overstate the evil effects of sentimental and emotional opinions and practices when young unconverted persons are exposed to them. The stern facts by which conviction is brought to the conscience are all but idealized; the true character of sin, and God's wrath against it, is overlooked or obscured; and while the death and resurrection of Christ are indeed spoken of, the full character of His work and His definite fulfillment of God's holy law for us in His life, are lost in a dreamy notion which in part at least puts His resurrection in the place of His death, as that by which the full atonement is made. In this manner devotional feelings are often stirred up; but without the primary ground having been cleared; without the question of sin and its forgiveness through the blood of the cross having been settled; and without the acceptance of the righteousness wrought out in the living obedience of Christ when on earth, as that in which the sinner can stand before God. Apparent devotedness is thus at times excited: there is the endeavor, on emotional grounds, to do much for God, but without the preliminary truth having been grasped of what, in the gift of Christ, God has done for us. There is in all this the endeavor to show good fruit from the tree which is still in its natural corruption. This, too, is often fostered by the misuse of devotional books, as if they could be substituted for coming to Christ in heart and conscience; and by the injudicious tone of "good books," which touch the feelings only, even when they are not replete with error of doctrine and principle.

The religion of sentiment and emotion often leads to mere asceticism: a very different thing from the practical holiness in which the believer is called on to walk. Any unconverted sentimentalist may assume an ascetic garb as a substitute for the Gospel.

It has been remarkable to notice how the sentimental expectation of the Lord's coming has led away from the close and reverential study of Holy Scripture. I0ndeed, it has been painful to hear earnest and real desire definitely to study the Word of God regarded and termed by some, as being "occupied with the letter of Scripture." (See Appendix J.) But do those who say this know what they mean? They speak of principles, and of having their minds occupied with Christ; but how do we obtain true principles except from God's revelation in the Word? and how does the Spirit lead the mind to be occupied with

The Hope of Christ's Second Coming

Christ, except from the definite truth of Holy Scripture? In fact, those who thus speak, putting the spirit in contrast to the letter, appear not to know what they are discussing; and as to Scripture itself, by paying but little heed to what they call "the letter," they really disregard so far what the Spirit has there set forth. "But oh! (they say) this head knowledge, this intellectual study of truth! How it leads our minds away from Christ!" It is true that there may be mental intelligence with but little spirituality; but it is equally true that if we obey God we shall never neglect the words of His Scripture.

Of course, with this tone of feeling, all critical study of Scripture is decried; it is deemed a waste of time. Even the study of the Word of God in the original Hebrew and Greek is spoken of as if it were a secular occupation. The English Bible is thought to be enough for teachers and taught alike; and thus they remain alike uninstructed. And if the original languages are looked at, exact scholarship is deemed superfluous. How different is this from the real study of God's Word; from using and valuing each portion, however minute, as being from Him, and as being that of which He can unfold to us the meaning by the teaching of His Spirit. How different from the practical application of the most definite rules of grammar, which lead to absolute persuasion that apostles and evangelists wrote nothing at random, but that even as to the most delicate shades of thought they used the right cases, moods, and tenses.[22] All diligent and careful inquiry, and

---

[22] "It is unwelcome news to the maintainer of some cherished exposition, to be told by an unsympathizing critic that it is a baseless vision, a notion unsupported by the language of the text. And it is also worthy of remark, how often the supporters of extravagancies in theology have manifested an

laborious examination of authorities, so as to know what were the very words in which the inspired writers gave forth the Scripture, is regarded as merely intellectual and secular. But is this a healthy tone of thought? Should not those who believe in the Divine authority of Holy Scripture know that they ought not to neglect its critical study? And if it be truly inspired, ought they not to feel that it is of some importance to inquire what is its true text—what, as far as existing evidence can show, were the very words in which the Holy Ghost gave it forth?[23]

Most difficult is it to arouse Christians in general to a sense of the full importance of critical study of Scripture; and especially is this the case when dreamy apprehensions are cherished, and where vague idealism has taken the place of truth, and sentimental asceticism is the substitute for Christian holiness.

There may be an external knowledge of Scripture where there is no spiritual life or light; but that is no reason for cherishing what is supposed to be spiritual in contrast to the words of inspiration. Such a contrast cannot really exist. He who truly loves the Lord Jesus Christ, and is guided by His Spirit, will be the most subject to that which is written in the Word. True

---

instinctive dread of exact learning." Rev. T. S. Green, M.A., *On the Grammar of the New Testament Dialect*. First Edition, 1842. Introduction, p. v.

[23] The opposition of visionary teachers and the receivers of their teaching to all textual criticism founded on evidence—to all investigation, in fact, regarding what are the real words and sentences given forth under the inspiration of the Holy Ghost—appears to be only equaled by the temerity with which, in certain cases, they accept conclusions which they desire, rather on assertion than on evidence.

The Hope of Christ's Second Coming

acquaintance with Scripture is the best check to mere sentimental emotion.[24]

---

[24] "This know also, that in the last days perilous times shall come: for men shall be lovers of their own selves....Having a form of godliness, but denying the power thereof: from such turn away. For of this sort are they which creep into houses, and lead captive silly women laden with sins, led away with divers lusts, ever learning and never able to come to the knowledge of the truth....But continue thou in the things which thou hast learned....All Scripture is given by inspiration of God, and is profitable for doctrine, for reproof, for correction, for instruction in righteousness; that the man of God may be perfect thoroughly furnished unto all good works." (2 Timothy 3). So taught the Apostle of the Gentiles, who was himself an able "minister of the New Testament" (2 Cor. 2:6), for the guidance of the Church in the "perilous times."

S. P. Tregelles

Chapter 23
'The Resurrection of the Just'

The doctrine of the Resurrection of the Just, even when held with but little apprehension of the events connected with that time, has always kept alive, as a fact, the reality of the coming of the Lord in power and great glory; for the expectation has not been some idealistic thought of Christ secretly taking His people to Himself, but His visible appearing, the visible opening of the graves, when "the dead shall be raised incorruptible, and we shall be changed." Is the hope of resurrection a mere personal expectation? Few, I suppose, would say this; for it is that in which the family of faith has a common hope and a common interest. But of which should we think most, in connection with it, the glory of Christ, or of our own blessedness? Surely the former: and this puts secrecy out of the question.

Even, too, as to ourselves, publicity is an essential part of the hope of resurrection; for in the resurrection of Christ's people, they shall be fully declared to be His, in body as well as in Spirit; and until then their triumph cannot be a manifested thing. The resurrection of Christ was His own personal vindication, as the One in whom the Father was ever well pleased—it defined and marked Him out as the Son of God, the Lord of all glory. But He shall yet be publicly vindicated. Up to this time, His believing people die and lie in their graves apparently as do others; their bodies are "sown in corruption," "in weakness," "in dishonor;" it seems, as to the bodies of the saints, that Satan has a triumph over them, and as if he could still dishonor Christ in His members. Whatever a secret resurrection might do for the blessedness of the saints themselves, it would not vindicate Christ in them; and He comes "to be glorified in His saints." Even if there could be a secret resurrection "in incorruption," yet a secret resurrection "in glory" (and it is in glory that the just shall be raised) would be a contradiction.

The death of a believer is great gain to him personally, for he departs to be with Christ, which is far better; but still it leaves him with an unconsummated hope; and in each case Christ has one more whose resurrection is needful for His own glory to be vindicated. We need feel no surprise at the prominence which the New Testament gives to resurrection; for although a part of the Church shall be alive and remain at the coming of the Lord, yet, as a fact, the great majority of Christians—the believers of long-succeeding age after age have fallen asleep; and thus, as to the Church in general,—it is not change, but resurrection which is the point of expectation. It may be said, that both these classes, the saints living when the Lord comes, and those in their graves, are needful for the manifestation of Christ as "the Resurrection and the Life." If all believers were to die, it would seem as if Christ had not so overcome death and Satan (who had the power of death) that He might lead His redeemed into glory without their passing through death. The change of the living saints when He comes shall show how in this He is "the Life." If all His people had lived on till His coming, it might have seemed as if theirs was but some protraction of existent natural life, and not the power of resurrection ministered to them. Christ died and lived, "that He might be Lord both of the dead and living" (Rom. 14:9). As Lord of the dead, He receives into blessing in His own presence (how joyful who can tell?) the spirits of His departed people: He cares for their moldering bodies, and He has pledged himself to raise them in "the last day." Then it shall be seen that He is "the Resurrection;" that of all the Father gave Him He hath lost nothing; and that His glory shall be manifested in the triumph of His members as sharers actually in that promised hope of resurrection which He set before them.

I have already shown, from Scripture (*The Hope of Christ's Second Coming*—Chapter 12), that the resurrection of the just shall take place at the time when the Lord again puts forth His hand to bless His ancient people Israel; and also (*The Hope of Christ's Second Coming*—Chapter 7) that the first resurrection cannot be until the last form of anti-Christian evil shall be ended by the coming of Christ in glory.[25] The order of resurrection

---

[25] Christ remains at the right hand of God the Father until the time when the Father puts all enemies to be His footstool: "Jehovah said unto my Lord, Sit thou at my right hand, until I make thine enemies thy footstool" (Psalm 110:1). Jehovah shall then send the rod of Christ's strength out of Zion: "Rule thou in the midst of thine enemies." He does not leave His place at the right hand of glory above (Matt. 26:64) until the Father has prepared the enemies to be His footstool: then Christ comes forth to act on the commission thus received; and then He puts forth His authority in subjecting all enemies to Himself, as set for that purpose by the Father. Then He reigns in bringing all into subjection. Those who hold that Christ will leave the right hand of God to receive His Church secretly, before the Father has prepared the foes to be His footstool (thus contradicting His words before the high priest),

The Hope of Christ's Second Coming

in 1 Corinthians 15 teaches the same thing: "Every man in his own order: Christ the first-fruits; afterward they that are Christ's at His coming. Then [i.e. afterwards, at a subsequent period in order] cometh the end, when He shall have delivered up the kingdom to God, even the Father....For He must reign until He have put all enemies under His feet" (1 Cor. 15:23–25). "They that are Christ's at His coming" are all saints up to that time—those who share in the first resurrection. "The end," spoken of as subsequent, is the period of the resurrection of Millennial saints, and of all others (though the just are only specifically treated of in this chapter). Thus, there can be no resurrection of "those that are Christ's" until the coming at which He restores Israel, and raises His believing people "in glory." "Thanks be to God, which giveth us the victory through our Lord Jesus Christ. Wherefore, my beloved brethren, be ye steadfast, unmoveable, always abounding in the work of the Lord;

---

have sometimes tried to render the passage in Psalm 110, and the citations of it in the New Testament, as though they meant "until I do set, or am setting," as if it were what He is about to do. Some have even gone the length of asserting that critically the notion is not that of the future perfect. A passage from Genesis, which was said to show this as to the Hebrew, was some years ago quoted and circulated in print; but for the sake of any puzzled by this, I mention, that the words quoted from Genesis were not his sentiment, but an opinion, the incorrectness of which he was showing, as any Hebrew scholar might do! It is wonderful that any one can say that the Greek in the New Testament can mean anything except "until I shall have placed thine enemies." The words "until He have put" are a similar construction, and any one can see that this is not "until He is putting;" the whole force of the argument turns on the thing having been done.

forasmuch as ye know that your labour is not in vain in the Lord."

Thus does the hope of resurrection in glory at Christ's appearing lead to true Christian service.

The Hope of Christ's Second Coming

S. P. Tregelles

Chapter 24
The Hope

Hope is always proposed to us for a definite object, and that of a kind which the hope should from its nature produce. The hope of the coming of the Lord, and our gathering to Him in glory, is given to the Church militant that it may be thereby strengthened for service and endurance. When the land on which Caleb had trodden was promised him for an inheritance, it was a hope that rested on his soul through the forty years' wandering in the wilderness, and during the conquest of the land, until he received it in the apportionment from Joshua; he was then fourscore and five years old, still kept alive by the Lord, and still as strong to go in and out for war as in the day that he had been sent by Moses to spy out the land. He did not expect the accomplishment of the hope until the forty years of judicial sojourn in the wilderness were completed until Jordan was crossed, and the land conquered. It was hope, though he knew of intervening years. When we are directed to look unto "Jesus, the author and finisher of our faith," it is as the One who had been Himself sustained by hope, "who for [or answerable to] the joy that was set before Him, endured the cross, despising the shame, and is set down at the right hand of the throne of God" (Heb. 12:2). So, too, as to us; it is as

The Hope of Christ's Second Coming

we have the hope set before us, rightly apprehended and sustained in the power of the Spirit of God, that we can serve and suffer.

Every time that believers meet around the Lord's table, to unite in the Lord's supper, as a part of the one Church, they declare, in obeying the Lord's command, that they unite in the Church's hope: "As oft as ye eat this bread, and drink this cup, ye do show the Lord's death till He come." The coming is that public coming which He taught: just as we look back at the one Cross, and the one work of atonement there wrought, so is the one hope professed, "that blessed hope: the appearing of the glory of our great God and Savior Jesus Christ." The hope can be as little turned into something ideal, or of sentiment and emotion merely, as can the solemn reality of the Cross, and its one finished work. Any hope but that which God has given might make ashamed: "We rejoice (says the Apostle) in hope of the glory of God" (Rom. 5:2). For hope resting on God's Word cannot "make ashamed." God's love to us is shed abroad in the heart by the Holy Ghost given unto us: so that a hope directed by Holy Scripture is one which cannot fail. The Church is taught to pray, "Our Father, which art in heaven....Thy kingdom come;" and this directs our thoughts and hopes onward (as it is surely intended to do) to that day when the Son of Man shall gather out of His kingdom all things that offend; and then (and not before) shall the righteous shine forth as the sun in the kingdom of their Father.[26]

---

[26] The advocates of the secret rapture well know that they are looking for what will (they suppose) be long prior to the kingdom; therefore do they put from them as their hope the Scriptures which speak of "the kingdom" and "the Gospel of the kingdom." But we are taught to pray, "Thy kingdom

S. P. Tregelles

Manifested glory is an essential part of our hope. So far is the hope of a secret or private removal of believers to the Lord from having that character, that it more resembles the expectation of being taken away by death: a secret translation would be different from death in its nature, but it would be equally contrary to the appearing of the Lord in glory. Death, it must be remembered, is nowhere set before us as our hope; for although the believer has hope in death, and a hope that triumphs over the power of death, the removal of our spirits to be with the Lord is greatly different from our hope. It is a mistake to suppose the coming of the Lord to mean death; for death is not our Lord, and death is ours as well as life; and in dying we go to Him instead of His coming to us. A very similar mistake is it to suppose a private taking of Christ's people to Him to be His coming in glory, for which we are called to wait.

An essential difference between the hope of the Lord's coming and death was long ago pointed out in this one particular: if we die, we leave the things here in their present course, and though our own life will be ended by death, yet the things in which we have taken an interest will not; and thus often, so far from the thought of death separating from worldly hopes, it has had the opposite

---

come;" and, lest this should be idealized, the next words are, "Thy will be done in earth, as it is in heaven." This is not the point to which those look who expect to be taken to the Lord, and that then there will be a period in which God's will shall be especially contravened on earth in all Satanic power and anti-Christian blasphemy. Therefore, such act consistently in abstaining from the use of the petitions of the Lord's Prayer. But we may know assuredly, that any theory or principle which sets aside a distinct command of Christ is thereby proved to be erroneous. We can thus test what seem to be refined forms of doctrine.

The Hope of Christ's Second Coming

effect of leading into arrangements for the continuance of those things in which pleasure was taken: they have been valued for the sake of persons left behind. The hope of a secret removal of the Church, without the hand of the Lord bringing all the present course of things to an end, may have, and has had, a similar effect. It has been thought that though the Church is removed, all secular things will remain, and that, as to them, arrangements might be made of the same kind as if removal by death were expected. Is this a hope that triumphs over present things and the snares of the world?[27]

There are, indeed, some who say, "An expectation of times of extreme peril before the Lord's coming, times of great tribulation, during which Christ's people would have to wait on this earth, would be no hope to me—it would only lead to discouragement and dismay: I want that which would animate my soul; no hope that is not of such a character would produce in me an emotion of present joy, or give me sustained comfort." Such reasoners go on sometimes to say, that even though proof of revealed events to occur before the coming of Christ is logically correct, although no flaw or fallacy can be detected in the arguments, yet because the result is such as cannot be accepted, therefore there must be a defect somewhere.[28]

---

[27] "My children are not yet converted (it has been actually said), therefore they have not the hope of the rapture of the Church; but as Christ may remove me as one of His people any day, I have to make proper provision for them and their position in this world."

[28] Such persons often escape from the bearing of Scriptures on their consciences by calling them "Jewish." But let such be asked, Do you mean "unbelieving-Jewish"? or "Christian-Jewish?" If they say the latter, then must the persons to whom such Scriptures apply be part of the Church, as

Therefore in meeting such thoughts, it is well that it is on testimony that we rest as to this truth; not on a process of reasoning, but on the inspired declarations which bear on this point on every side.

But will the expectations produce no animating hope? Will there be no emotions according to God from the thought of seeing Christ in His glory, and being like Him at His coming? It is not on the intervening darkness that we have to rest, but on the brightness beyond; that is our hope, and it is made known to us that we may understand our place of service and patience while waiting for the coming of our Lord, by which all trial shall be for ever ended. However hopeless it may be to meet the arguments of idealistic visionaries, who assume a conclusion, and refuse to submit to opposing Scripture testimony, yet for others it is well distinctly to show that the hope of Christ's coming was given to be the sustainment and consolation in intervening trial. So far from its being a thing to cast down or depress, it is gracious in the Lord to have told us what to expect in the path of the Church up to the time of the appearing of Jesus Christ.

The Apostle Peter, in his first epistle, contemplates Christians as "begotten again unto a lively hope by the resurrection of Jesus Christ from the dead" (1 Peter 1:3), while waiting for the "inheritance incorruptible, and undefiled, and that fadeth not away, reserved in heaven for you who are kept by the power of God, through faith unto salvation, ready to be revealed in the last time" (1 Peter 1:

---

essentially so as the Ephesians were; if they say the former, then it may be asked them, How can unconverted Jews use any part of the New Testament at all? If an expression be adopted, and used without explanation or definition, it may then afford a shelter for any ambiguity or fallacy.

4,5). Meanwhile, such may be "in heaviness through manifold temptations; that the trial of your faith, being much more precious than of gold that perisheth, though it be tried with fire, might be found unto praise, and honor, and glory at the appearing [revelation] of Jesus Christ" (1 Peter 1:7). The trial may be borne, the temptations may be endured, as knowing what the blessing shall be at the revelation of the Lord Himself. And what is the practical exhortation to those thus set in the place of present trial: "Wherefore gird up the loins of your mind; be sober, and hope to the end for the grace that is to be brought unto you at the revelation of Jesus Christ" (1 Peter 1:13). This, then, is the point at which we are to look beyond all suffering, and this is the truth, as applied to our souls by the Spirit of God, which is to give us present sustainment. But, lest any should imagine that the Church should be exempt from special and peculiar times of suffering, as well as that which falls on men in general, he says, "Beloved, think it not strange concerning the fiery trial which is to try you, as though some strange thing happened unto you; but rejoice, inasmuch as ye are partakers of Christ's sufferings; that, when His glory shall be revealed, ye may be glad also with exceeding joy" (1 Peter 4:12,13). "Let them that suffer according to the will of God, commit the keeping of their souls unto Him in well doing, as unto a faithful Creator" (1 Peter 4:19). So also as to service. To those who feed the flock of God, taking oversight, the promise is, "When the Chief Shepherd shall appear, ye shall receive a crown of glory that fadeth not away" (1 Peter 5:4).

The Apostle James teaches us not only the need of patience in waiting for the Lord's coming, but that that hope is our power in continuous patience: "Be patient, therefore, brethren unto the coming of the Lord. Behold, the husbandman waiteth for the precious fruit of the earth, and hath long patience for it, until he receive the early and the latter rain. Be ye also patient; stablish your hearts; for the coming of the Lord draweth nigh" (James 5:7,8).

The Apostle Peter, in his second epistle, while instructing the Church as to events which would take place, and how they were to be guided after his decease, gives the practical directions how they should be occupied with the prophetic Word until the Lord comes: "We have also a more sure word of prophecy" ("the prophetic word more abiding" than the voice in the holy mount had been), "whereunto ye do well that ye take heed [until the day dawn and the day-star arise][29] in your hearts" (1 Peter

---

[29] The reasons for regarding "until the day dawn and the day-star arise" as a parenthetic clause, and for connecting "in your hearts" with what has gone before ("take heed in your hearts") are very strong; for what sense is there in the day-star arising in your hearts? If it meant any attainment in us, then it would indicate when we could do without the Scripture. The only tolerable objection that I have heard to the verse being thus read is, that προσέχω in this sense is an elliptical phrase for προσέχω τὸν νοῦν, and that thus ἐν ταῖς καρδίαις is a most unsuitable addition. But, first, an elliptical phrase is often so used that the ellipsis could not be supplied without encumbering the sentence; and, second, "in your hearts" is a kind of adverbial expression equivalent to "inwardly." We may be told to direct our minds inwardly to Holy Scripture, because it needs that it be inwardly digested. "In your hearts" is similarly an adverbial expression in 1 Peter 3:15, "Sanctify the Lord Christ in your hearts" ("inwardly sanctify Him"); if, indeed, there is not there a parenthesis, "Be not afraid of their terror, neither be troubled [but sanctify the Lord Christ] in your hearts." 1 Peter 3:21 is an instance of an expression remaining at the end of a parenthesis, connected in sense and construction with what has gone before: "save...by the resurrection of Jesus Christ" belong

1:19). Thus it is to the prophetic Scripture that we are directed; and he who feels the force of this injunction, and apprehends the authority of Scripture as given forth by the Holy Ghost, will feel that no diligence, no pains can be too great to be bestowed upon that which God has so given us, and about which He tells us that we "do well to take heed." Those whose hearts are subject to this commandment will not call the careful study of Scripture "mere head knowledge," "knowledge of the letter," or anything of the kind; they will seek to know what God has said, knowing that all Holy Scripture has been written for our learning, and for the reason that the Apostle gives immediately after: "Holy men of God spake as they were moved by the Holy Ghost;" and so far from feeling that their hope is dimmed thereby, they will know that they are waiting for Christ according to His word and will. To such the prophetic word will be indeed a light; and though darkness be around, they will be guided by that lamp which the Holy Ghost has kindled, until the day dawn and the day-star arise, until the glorious appearing of Him who is "the bright and morning star." Substitute a secret coming for the appearing of Jesus, and the prophetic word is no guide at all; for what bearing can prophecy have on the walk of those who ought not (on that theory) to be informed of a single event that can occur previous to the imagined secret rapture? Not such, however, is the teaching of apostles and prophets.

In the second and third chapters of this epistle, the Apostle gives ample warning of evils that should be. When men ask, "Where is the promise of His coming?" those

---

together; while "not the putting away of the filth of the flesh, but the answer of a good conscience before God," is simply a parenthetic statement.

who are instructed in Scripture may point to those testimonies which show what is to be expected, and why, in mercy to those who shall be gathered in, that day has not yet come. "We, according to His promise, look for new heavens and a new earth, wherein dwelleth righteousness" (2 Peter 3:13). We wait then "according to His promise." If the millennial blessing of Jerusalem and the people of Israel (Isa. 65:17,18) is an exemplification of the new heaven and earth thus promised, how much there is in which the prophetic word may cause us to rejoice as to the glories of the reign of Christ. If we look for the new heavens and new earth, this is to us an object of hope; but it is one which cannot be immediate; for not till Christ has put down all authority and power, not till all enemies are subjected to Him, and even till death, the last enemy, has been destroyed, can there be the new heaven and the new earth. Thus we hope for Christ's glorious coming, we hope for the millennial reign which then begins, and we hope onward for that which is thus postmillennial (Rev. 21:1–8), when "God shall be all in all." We see before us point after point of glory and blessedness revealed, "according to His promise." "Wherefore, beloved, seeing that ye look for such things, be diligent that ye be found of Him in peace without spot and blameless." (2 Peter 3:14.) "Ye, therefore, beloved, seeing ye know before [the warnings given of intervening evil], beware lest ye also, being led away with the error of the wicked, fall from your own steadfastness" (2 Peter 3:17).

Most close is the connection between prophecy and promise. Prophecy is to the believer often promise: thus in Heb. 12:26, "Now He hath promised, saying, Yet once more I shake not the earth only, but also heaven." Where is this promise written? In Haggai 2:6, we find the prophecy, which to the child of faith is promise, because it

The Hope of Christ's Second Coming

has to do with that day when the "kingdom which cannot be moved" shall be ours, in contrast to all that can pass away. The same epistle had before taught, "Ye have need of patience, that after ye have done the will of God, ye might receive the promise. For yet a little while, and He that shall come will come, and will not tarry" (Heb. 10:36,37). The appearing of the Lord is to manifest His triumph in the Gospel: "As it is appointed unto men once to die, and after this the judgment; so Christ was once offered to bear the sins of many; and unto them that look for Him shall He appear the second time, without sin, until salvation" (Heb. 9:27,28).[30]

The Epistles of Peter and James, and that to the Hebrews, are parts of Scripture which some term "Jewish;" but are they not markedly Christian? Does not the hope of Christ's appearing, as set forth in them, lead to Christian walk and acting? Ought not patience, service, and hope to characterize all Christians? But these are some of the graces here set forth as results of a true apprehension of the coming of Christ. So, too, is the diligent study of God's Word, and the upholding of its authority. There have been previously quoted many passages from the epistles of St. Paul to Gentile churches or to individuals: is not the consolation concerning the departed a precious part of our hope? Is it a light thing to be called always to abound in the work of the Lord? Is ability to glory in tribulations of small importance? And yet all these are connected with the

---

[30] Men, as men, have before them death as the wages of sin, and after that the judgment: believers instead of having death thus as the penalty to fall on them, look back to the cross where Christ bore their sins; instead of looking on to judgment, they look to the coming of Christ for salvation in its fullest and most ample sense.

hope of the appearing, the manifest revelation of Christ, and with nothing previous, and with nothing secret. Imagine a secret coming, and then how will any of these precepts and principles apply?

So far as there is found in the holders of the secret advent a power of Christian hope, love, service, joy, and endurance, so far does it spring, not from their theory, but from the measure of truth with which the soul is directed to Christ as the One who shall come. God sometimes works graciously on souls, in spite of very defective apprehensions of truth; but how much more could they act according to Him if their hopes were rightly directed.

The Apostle John teaches us: "Beloved, now are we the sons of God, and it doth not yet appear what we shall be; but we know that, when He shall appear, we shall be like Him, for we shall see Him as He is; and every man that hath THIS HOPE in Him [i.e. resting on Christ—ἐπ'αὐτῷ] purifieth himself, even as He is pure" (1 John 3:2,3).

This, then, is the practical power of the hope of Christ's manifestation: this it is that can enable believers to glorify Him who has cleansed them in His blood, and clothed them in His righteousness: this it is that sets before them that consummation in which Christ shall be glorified, in His people receiving the full results of His redemption. This Scripture answers any who ask, "What effect can the hope of Christ's appearing have? and why should such an expectation be cherished as a holy hope? Then it is that we shall be like Him. It is not a deduction, not a conclusion in which there may be some mistake; but the definite statement of the Holy Ghost in His own inspired Scripture. If we believe the promises of God as He has set them forth, we shall not transfer to a secret coming of Christ the many things and the practical results which the Scripture joins to His appearing in glory. It is better to act implicitly on what God says, even when we understand not His objects: still more should we do this when He tells us why He teaches us, when He seeks to make known to us His counsels, and intelligently to guide our souls by the promise of that revelation of Christ; then all who have been partakers of grace shall fully show the efficacy of His blood of atonement, and then shall they reign with Him in His manifested glory.

"He which testifieth these things saith, Surely I come quickly: Amen. Even so, come, Lord Jesus."

— Plymouth, March 17, 1864

S. P. Tregelles

Appendix A:
The Jewish 'Waste-paper Basket'

It is a sad but significant fact that this view has been logically developed since the above words were written. It is well known that numbers of persons holding these opinions about the "Jewish" character of the instruction conveyed in the Gospels, have ceased to practice baptism "in the Name of the Father, the Son, and the Holy Ghost," solely on the ground that its institution in these terms is recorded only in the Gospels, substituting for it "baptism in the name of the Lord Jesus," which, they say, is true Christian baptism according to the full Church—standing revealed first in the Acts. Within my own personal knowledge persons have refused to accept baptism if administered in the Name of the Trinity, on the alleged ground that this would not be true Christian baptism; and I have been told that the command to go forth and baptize in that manner was only intended to apply to the labors of the apostles before the day of Pentecost, and again, after having been suspended during the term they distinguish as the Church period (i.e., the period extending from Pentecost to the so-called future secret rapture of the saints), to come into operation during the interval supposed to elapse between that removal of the Church and the manifestation of the Lord in glory. And,

The Hope of Christ's Second Coming

as regards the Lord's Supper, I am personally acquainted with the case of at least one professed teacher who, with his followers, has openly abandoned that ordinance on the ground that, having been instituted in the Gospels, it is virtually a Jewish ordinance.

Appendix B: Analogies

These efforts seem to be increasingly made. The most dangerous examples of the principle are found in its application to the interpretation of prophetic parables. For example, it has been urged in my hearing that in the parable of the wise and foolish virgins (Matthew 25), the wise virgins cannot possibly represent the Church, because the Church is elsewhere described in Scripture as "the Bride," and in this parable the Bride is conspicuous by her absence! It is evident that if arguments are to be founded upon what is not stated in parables, they may be expounded to mean anything, according to the will or fancy of the expounder.

THE HOPE OF CHRIST'S SECOND COMING

S. P. Tregelles

Appendix C:
Jewish Aspects of the Tribulation in Palestine

It is frequently assumed that the Lord's words, "Pray ye that your flight be not...on the Sabbath" (Matt. 24:20), unmistakably show that those addressed are Jews, it being supposed that they are regarded as persons who would be bound by the law of the Sabbath, and thereby prevented from journeying upon that day. It is, however, abundantly clear from the conjoined phrase, "in the winter," and the words of the nineteenth verse, that the Lord's object is not to release them from the difficulty of disobedience to the Mosaic law of the Sabbath, but to avert certain sufferings from the hand of man which would come upon them if they attempted to carry out on the Sabbath His command to flee from Jerusalem. The truth is that the persons addressed are Christians, in faith and standing like ourselves (as, indeed, is necessarily implied in their being disciples of the Lord Jesus, in which character they are instructed in this chapter), who will be resident in Jerusalem at the time when "the abomination of desolation" shall be set "in the holy place," as predicted by Daniel (cf. Matt. 24:15 with Dan. 9:27 marg.), and who are commanded to flee immediately from the land. If they

The Hope of Christ's Second Coming

had to flee during winter, or as described in verse 19, great sufferings would be entailed by the circumstances of the journey; and in mercy they are permitted to pray for the providential adjustment of those circumstances as to the season of the year, etc. But it must also be remembered that at the time contemplated, Israel, as a people, will have been regathered into the Holy Land, the temple rebuilt (otherwise there would be no "holy place" to be invaded by the "abomination of desolation"), and the ordinances of the Mosaic code re-established as the law of the land. One of these, the law of the Sabbath (cf. John 11:18 and Acts 1:12), restricted journeying on that day; and is clearly viewed as in operation. To violate it, therefore, would entail on the Lord's disciples the wrath of a fanatical people inflamed by a zeal like that which hindered them from entering Pilate's judgment hall lest they should be defiled, while they were clamoring for the murder of the Holy One and the Just. Matthew 12:1–14 may be instructively compared.

S. P. Tregelles

Appendix D:
Five Aspects of the Kingdom of God

In their attempts to divert the application of this parable from the saints of this dispensation, the advocates of the secret rapture plead that the word "kingdom" shows at once that the professing Church is not contemplated as the "wheat" and "tares," for, say they, "the Church is not the kingdom." The reply is, that although the Church is not the kingdom in the sense of being strictly coextensive with it, yet it forms a part of the kingdom of God, for to be in the true Church is to be in the kingdom; as is shown by the words of the Apostle in Col. 1:13, "who hath translated us into the kingdom of His dear Son."

The subject will be simplified if we remember that "the kingdom of God" is viewed in Scripture under five different aspects:

1. As introduced into the world in the person of the Lord Jesus Christ, its King and Head. See Mark 1:14,15, where "is at hand" should be rendered "hath drawn nigh" (ἤγγικεν).

2. As rejected by Israel, and therefore restricted—during this dispensation of evil in which Satan and "the rulers of the darkness of this world" guide the course of the age—to a body of men whose relationship to

it is invisible, and only manifested by their subjection to its laws and principles. But this body of men forms what we know as the Church, the body of Christ. Now as the Gospel brings into this relationship those who believe, it follows that "to testify the Gospel of the grace of God" is equivalent to "preaching the kingdom of God" (See Acts 20:24,25).

3. In that outward visible aspect, in which, during this dispensation, it includes all who profess to belong to the Lord Jesus Christ—some truly, some falsely. It is, in this aspect, exactly equivalent to what is commonly described by the word "Christendom" (i.e. Christ's kingdom), that it is spoken of in Matthew 23.

4. In the future, or millennial aspect, when the government of the Lord Jesus Christ will be manifested in power. The kingdom will then include (a) a heavenly department, the Risen "Church of the first-born ones" (Heb. 12); and (b) an earthly department, consisting of Israel as a converted people, and also the converted Gentiles throughout the earth. It is in this aspect that we pray "Thy kingdom come: Thy will be done on earth as in heaven."

5. In the eternal aspect, as in the words "then cometh the end, when He [the Son] shall deliver up the kingdom to God, even the Father," etc. (1 Cor. 15:24).

S. P. Tregelles

Appendix E: Responsibility for False Teaching

This responsibility is a very heavy one. It is no light thing to undertake the instruction of others in the truth of God. The words of St. James are very solemn: "My brethren, be not many [of you] teachers (διδάσκαλοι), knowing that we shall receive the greater condemnation."

THE HOPE OF CHRIST'S SECOND COMING

S. P. Tregelles

Appendix F: 'A Thief in the Night'

In this connection it may be well to point out the force of the passages which speak of the Lord's coming "as a thief in the night," which, we are constantly told, prove that the Lord intends His true saints to regard His advent as momentarily imminent. Such passages occur at Matt. 24:43; Luke 12:39,40; 1 Thess. 5:2; 2 Peter 3:10; and, Rev. 16:15. With regard to them all, it may be remarked that the emblem of "a thief" is obviously used to indicate not merely the unexpectedness of the coming, but its unwelcomeness! Further, this emblem implies the advent of one who comes to take away, not to give something to those whom he visits, for "the thief cometh not but for to steal, to kill, and to destroy." These considerations are surely sufficient by themselves to show at the first glance that it is not the Lord's coming in its relation to the true believer, to him who "loves His appearing," and to whom "grace shall be brought at the revelation of Jesus Christ," that is indicated, but its relation to the false professor of the Name of Jesus, the "evil servant," whose words in the parable, "My lord delayeth his coming," show that he neither expected his lord's return nor desired it. But the point is not one of inference, however clear: the passage in 1 Thess. 5:4 says with the utmost plainness that the coming of the Lord "as a thief" does not bear this character to His people, but to those who are "in darkness;" for when they shall say peace and safety," etc. "But ye, brethren, are not in darkness that that day should overtake you as a thief."

The passage in Luke 12 deserves special study. The Lord speaks first of the watchfulness of His true people (Luke 12:35–38). Next, we find a hint that there will be some to whom His return will be unwelcome (Luke 12:39, 40). With an immediate apprehension of the fact that two differing classes of persons must be under mention, Peter puts the inquiry of verse 41. The answer makes it clear that two classes were intended; the "wise steward" (Luke 12:42–44) and "that [other] servant" (Luke 12:45–48), the representative of the false professing Church. There is a clear connection between the words "when ye think not" (Luke 12:40) and "when he looketh not for him" (Luke 12:46). The Lord does not place before His true, loving, faithful servants His advent as an event to occur at an hour when they think not: these words of caution, though spoken to all, are intended only for the "tares" that Satan has mingled with the "wheat." It is the rule in Scripture, in dealing with mixed bodies, to address words of warning to all, which are only meant to apply to some of those addressed, it being left to the individual conscience to make the application (compare Heb. 6:4–9).

S. P. Tregelles

Appendix G:
Remarks on and Summary of the Apocalypse

By Cecil Yates Biss

This argument assumes that the chapters of the Revelation follow one another in a chronological sequence, so that what is narrated in Chapter 4 (the vision of the crowned elders) must be fulfilled long before that which is recorded in Chapter 19, viz. the appearing in glory of the Lord. This assumption, however, is a fallacy, as a very brief examination of the matter will show. The order of narration is not historical but moral; that which occurs last being often here (as elsewhere) narrated first. Indeed, it is usual in all prophetic Scripture to exhibit the final scene of triumph and glory—"the preface of blessing," as it has been most appropriately called—before the intervening development of evil and of judgment. A conspicuous example is found in the second chapter of Isaiah, which contains the first of the visions granted to that prophet. The first five verses present a glorious picture of the final blessing of Israel in the millennial day, followed by a terrible description of the judgments which shall precede the Day of the Lord and the humbling of the nation under His hand.

Furthermore, the Revelation, like other books of prophecy, is composed of a series of visions which present, in different aspects and with varying details, the events of the same, or parts of the same period of history, the rule being that the earlier visions give outlines, the later ones details, of the same events. There is not the slightest difficulty in perceiving that after the vision of the glory of the risen saints in heaven given in Chapters 4 and 5 of the Revelation, Chapter 6 gives an outline which reaches to the close of the present dispensation, treating, in fact, of the same events as are related in different connections, in Chapter 19.

That the vision presented in Chapters 4, 5 is anticipative is proved by the fact that coincidentally with the worship in heaven of the crowned elders and living ones representing the risen saints, the earth at large, and Israel in it, are presented in relations of millennial blessing. The words "they reign on the earth" (Chapter 5, 10) which Dr. Tregelles asserts, form the true reading (see *ante*, note on p. 91) must point to Israel enjoying the fulfillment of Isa. 60:8–12. And even if the saints on earth, whose prayers are presented before the throne by the crowned elders in heaven, could be supposed to be the Remnant of Israel during the days of anti-Christian tribulation (a supposition full of the most irreconcilable difficulties, but which has been strongly urged), it is impossible to overlook the fact that the earth with all its inhabitants (verse 13) is represented as joining, at the same time, in the song of praise to God and the Lamb. This could never take place until the period of anti-Christian evil was over, and the Lord was exalted throughout the earth (see Psalm 46, 47), that is, until after His second advent.

And yet it is frequently urged that "the structure of the Revelation" is the strongest argument for the rapture of the saints at a secret coming occurring some time prior to the Lord's appearing in glory!

It will be easily seen by the following outline of the Revelation, that the principle of repetition is followed throughout that book, as indeed is the case, generally, in all the prophetic Scriptures.

Chapter 1—General introduction.

Chapter 2, 3—The decline and approaching judgment of corporate Gentile Christianity, as represented by the Seven Churches of Asia.

Chapter 4, 5—A vision of the heavenly glory of the risen "Church of the first-born," and the Millennial blessing of the earth; forming the "preface of blessing" to the Revelation as a whole.

Chapter 6—A vision, in outline, of the judgments immediately preceding the Lord's advent. The "preface of blessing" is given in verse 2, where the Lord is displayed as the Conqueror; after which the chapter retraces the narration, giving instruction regarding points prior to His appearing.

Chapter 7–9—A section giving fuller details of the Divine judgments which precede the Advent. The "preface of blessing" is given in Chapter 7, which sets forth the two elect bodies who are preserved for blessing at that period; first, The Elect Remnant of Israel (Chapter 7:1–8); and, second, "The Church of the first-born ones which are written in Heaven" (cf. Heb. 12:23).

Chapter 10-13—A section giving still fuller details of the same judgments, but restricted to the last 1,260 days of the dispensation, i.e. the last "half-week" of Daniel

The Hope of Christ's Second Coming

(Dan. 9:27). Hence this portion of the Revelation is called "a little book." The plan of the chapters is as follows: Chapter 10—The "preface of blessing"—a vision of the Lord's coming in power and glory. Chapter 11—Jerusalem's history during the 1,260 days' testimony of the two witnesses. Chapter 12—Christianity outcast and persecuted. Chapter 13—Antichrist reigning supreme.

Chapter 14—A vision enlarging certain of the points before mentioned, such as the testimony, sufferings, and blessed hope of the persecuted saints. The "preface of blessing" is in verses 1–5.

Chapter 15–18—A section dealing specially with the judgment of Babylon. Chapter 15—The "preface of blessing:" a vision of the Millennial glory and reign of Christ and His saints. Chapter 16—Judgments upon "the seat of the Beast and all who follow him." Chapter 17—Moral Babylon: (The anti-Christian system.) Chapter 18—Material Babylon: (The capital city of Antichrist's dominion.)

Chapter 19—The coming of the Lord in glory.

Chapter 20—The Millennial Reign, closed by a final revolt against God: the final judgment of the wicked dead.

Chapter 21:1–8—The New Heavens and Earth—Eternity.

Chapter 21:9—End.

Chapter 22. 1–5—The Heavenly City, in its relations with the Earth during the Millennium (The proof of this is seen in 22:2—"the leaves of the tree were for the healing of the nations." In the New Heaven and New Earth (21:1) there is no more curse, sorrow, crying, nor pain, "for the former things have passed away").

Chapter 22:6 to end—Concluding words of warning and promise.

S. P. Tregelles

Appendix H
Job Loved 'The Appearing'

Do not the words of Job (19:25–27) prove that he was truly one of those who, though from "afar off" (Heb. 11:13), discerned and loved the appearing of the Lord?

THE HOPE OF CHRIST'S SECOND COMING

S. P. Tregelles

Appendix J:
The "Theory" Leads Away From Close Bible Study

Error is always inconsistent. It should be remembered, as a warning, that those who speak thus have formulated the theory (refuted in detail at pp. 55,56) of the secret coming of the Lord as distinguished from His public appearing, founded upon the supposed distinction between the use of two Greek words! a distinction which (even if it were true) would be necessarily totally invisible to the ordinary reader, inasmuch as these words are not uniformly rendered by the same terms respectively, in the English version.

Nothing could be more palpably incorrect than to set the "letter" and "spirit" of Scripture in contrast. Nothing could be a greater error of exposition than to assert that 2 Cor. 3:6 (the passage from which these terms are derived) supports, or even suggests such a view. For "the letter which killeth" is the law of Sinai, "written and engraven in stones," and ministering death to sinful creatures—"the Spirit which giveth life" is that ministration of spiritual power acting through Christ, presented in the New Covenant as "the quickening Spirit" (1 Cor. 15:45), the antitype of the brazen serpent, which

The Hope of Christ's Second Coming

brings eternal life into the souls of all who believe on His name.

S. P. Tregelles

QUICK ORDER FORM

The Hope of Christ's Second Coming: How Is It Taught in Scripture? And Why?

A reprint of the classic analysis of the new "secret rapture" doctrine by the nineteenth century theologian and biblical scholar Samuel P. Tregelles, published in 1864.

148 pages. $12.95.

Copies   _____
Total Merchandise: $ _____
USPS Media Mail shipping included

Please send check or money order to:

Strong Tower Publishing
P.O. Box 973
Milesburg, PA 16853

For credit card orders:

Strong Tower Publishing will accept credit card orders through PayPal. Send payment to: strongtowerpubs@aol.com.

Pricing good through 2007.

For updated shipping and pricing information, visit our Web site at www.strongtowerpublishing.com.

www.ingramcontent.com/pod-product-compliance
Lightning Source LLC
Chambersburg PA
CBHW051803040426
42446CB00007B/498